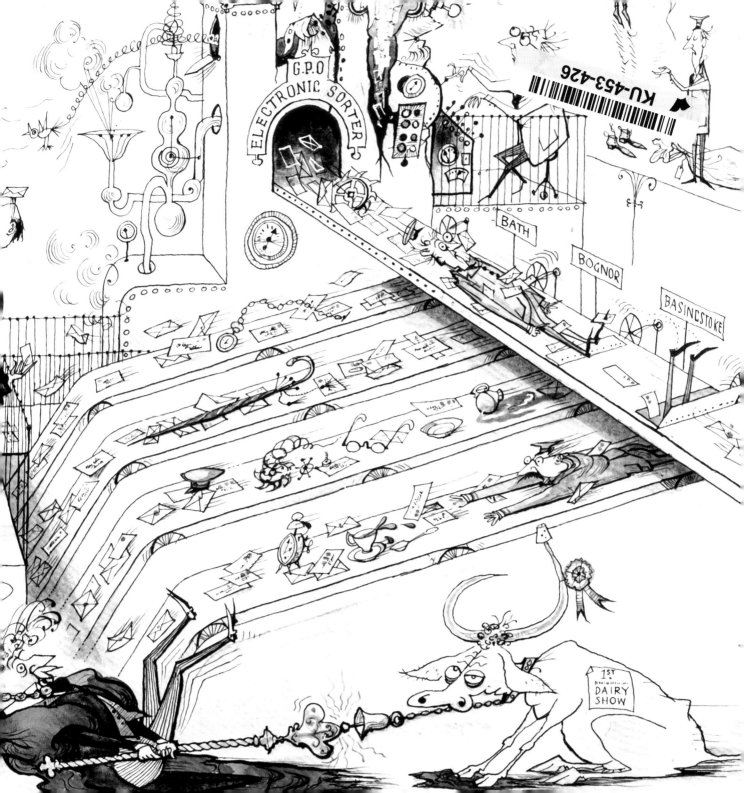

Copyright © Chris Beetles Ltd 2022
8 & 10 Ryder Street
St James's
London SW1Y 6QB
020 7839 7551
gallery@chrisbeetles.com
www.chrisbeetles.com

ISBN 978-1-914906-05-3
Cataloguing in publication data is available
from the British Library

A Chris Beetles Gallery Publication

With contributions by Chris Beetles, Alexander Beetles,
Phoebe Ross and David Wootton
Edited by Alexander Beetles, Fiona Nickerson and Pascale Oakley

Design by Fiona Nickerson and Pascale Oakley

Photography by Alper Goldenberg and Julian Huxley-Parlour
Reproduction by www.cast2create.com
Colour separation and printing by Geoff Neal Litho Limited

**Dedicated to Ed Koren, the great *New Yorker*
cartoonist and friend of the gallery**

Front cover:
Edward Ardizzone, *The Bar Maid* [**129**]

Front endpaper:
Rowland Emett, *A Harrowing Prospect of Mount Pleasant* [**147**]

This page:
Mabel Lucie Attwell, *I'm hoping good fairies are well on the way
To bring you good fortune for every day* [**95**]

Title page:
Kate Greenaway, *Study of a Young Girl with a Feathered Bonnet,
Cream Skirt and Brown Jacket* [**17**]

Back endpaper:
Paul Cox, *The Warrington Hotel* [**309**]

Back cover:
Henry Matthew Brock, *Hop O' My Thumb* [**49**]

THE ILLUSTRATORS

THE BRITISH ART OF ILLUSTRATION 1871-2022

CHRIS BEETLES GALLERY

8 & 10 Ryder Street, St James's, London SW1Y 6QB

020 7839 7551 gallery@chrisbeetles.com

www.chrisbeetles.com

CONTENTS

The Cartoonists of *Punch*

THE CARTOONISTS OF PUNCH

Punch, founded in 1841, was the Victorian periodical with consistently the funniest and most finely drawn cartoons. However, its own identity did not remain static, and evolved through to the turn of the century. Though initially radical, it increasingly communicated establishment values, a reform led in many ways less by the writers than by the cartoonists, a more essentially conservative body.

John Leech was the first significant cartoonist for *Punch*, and his drawings soon became one of the chief reasons for reading the periodical. One of his early contributions (satirising designs for murals for the new Houses of Parliament) even introduced the modern definition of 'cartoon' as a comic drawing.

Leech was more memorable in social than political subjects. The work he published was affectionately satirical about those he knew and understood, the middle classes at home and abroad and in 1851, he was joined at *Punch* by **John Tenniel**. It was John Tenniel whose dynamism helped change *Punch* from a run of the mill comic paper into a National Institution.

Certainly, Tenniel's specific talents as a draughtsman gave gravity to the style and the content of the periodical. He had harboured ambitions to be a history painter, and he brought the language of history painting to cartooning. His classical allegorical images took the long view of history and abstracted it. This is not to suggest that Tenniel lacked graphic energy or incisiveness, for his technique injected allegory with new potency. Neither was his work for *Punch* opposed to the spirit of that of Leech, or of Leech's successors as social cartoonists: **Charles Keene**, who was also employed from 1851, and **George Du Maurier**, who was employed from 1864. Rather, the two approaches worked together, the social cartoonist focussing on the small changes of fashions and manners, and the political cartoonist tending to reject the greater changes. And all tended to conservativism, instilling the sympathetic reader with confidence.

The cartoons in this chapter most strongly represent the *Punch* of the 1870s and 1880s, when its visual ethos was controlled by the triumvirate of Tenniel, Keene and Du Maurier. With the death of Keene in 1891 that would come to an end.

On the whole, they divided the world successfully between themselves into the three sectors of ordinary life, high society and politics. Such a distinct division of experience, aping a class system, was very much intrinsic to the establishment vision. Ordinary life (as depicted by Keene) was the acceptable arena for the joke with its often localised and instantly recognisable archetypes. High society (as satirised by Du Maurier) was the milieu of snobbery, jingoism and dilettantism. Politics (as defined by Tenniel) was the ideal realm of the grand and reassuring depictions of Empire and Parliamentary strife.

JOHN TENNIEL
Sir John Tenniel, RI (1820-1914)

While best remembered as the illustrator of Lewis Carroll's *Alice* books, John Tenniel contributed greatly to the look of *Punch* during the later nineteenth century. Beautifully drawn and highly allusive, his political cartoons remain startling in presenting fantastic imagery with classical polish.

John Tenniel was born at 22 Gloucester Place, New Road, Bayswater, London, on 28 February 1820, the third son among six children of John Baptist Tenniel, a fencing and dancing master of Huguenot origins, and his wife, Eliza (née Foster). Brought up in Kensington, he was educated locally and then by his father, before studying at the Royal Academy Schools. In 1840, despite being partially blinded by his father in a fencing accident, he continued in his ambition to be a history painter and joined the Clipstone Street Artists' Society (later known as the Langham Sketching Club) to increase his chances of exposure. Together with Charles Keene, a sketching companion at the Clipstone Academy, he created 'The Book of Beauty' (circa 1846), an unpublished parody of popular anthologies of engravings and verse. He rose to notice through his animal drawings, and attracted the attention of Mark Lemon, the editor of *Punch*, with his illustrations to the Rev Thomas James's edition of *Aesop's Fables* (1848). He joined the magazine as second cartoonist to John Leech in November 1850 and, becoming principal cartoonist in 1864, produced over 2,000 cartoons in 50 years. As the one Conservative member of staff, he defined the cartoon for the Empire through his development of stock types and patriotic symbols, while his early ambitions as an actor and a history painter enriched his imagery.

Tenniel married Julia Giani in 1854, and they settled at 10 Portsdown Road, Maida Hill. However, she died of tuberculosis only two years later and he never remarried.

Parallel to his position as a leading cartoonist, Tenniel developed his career as a book illustrator and made best use of his rich vein of fantasy in his work for Lewis Carroll: *Alice's Adventures in Wonderland* (1865) and *Through the Looking-Glass and What Alice Found There* (1872). He was elected to both the associate and full membership of the Institute of Painters in Water Colours in 1874, and was knighted in 1893. Tenniel's single most famous cartoon, concerning the dismissal of Bismarck and entitled *Dropping the Pilot*, appeared in *Punch* on 29 March 1890. Two years later, he gave up his practice of drawing directly on the engraving block and took to photographic reproduction. He retired from *Punch* at the age of 80, and in 1909 moved with his sister, Victoria, to a flat at 52 FitzGeorge Avenue, West Kensington. He died there on 25 February 1914. *Punch* produced a special commemorative issue on 4 March of that year, which was the date of his funeral.

His work is represented in numerous public collections, including the British Museum and the V&A; and New York Public Library.

Further reading:
L Perry Curtis Jnr, 'Tenniel, Sir John (1820-1914)', H C G Matthew and Brian Harrison (eds), *Oxford Dictionary of National Biography*, Oxford University Press, 2004, vol 54, pages 131-134;
Rodney Engen, *Sir John Tenniel: Alice's White Knight*, London: Scolar Press, 1991;
Roger Simpson, *Sir John Tenniel: Aspects of His Work*, Cranbury: Associated University Presses, 1994

Front cover of Sir John Tenniel's Cartoons from "Punch" 1871-1890

Photograph of Sir John Tenniel, circa 1880s

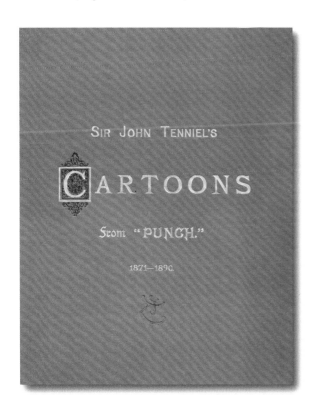

The cartoon as it appeared in *Punch* in 1871

THE REAL 'AUTUMN SESSION'

The coming of Autumn traditionally marks the start of the hunting season in England and Scotland, when the shooting of birds such as partridge and duck is permitted. In this cartoon, Mr Punch takes two fictitious members of the Commons and Lords on a shoot as a leisurely alternative to 'murdering bills at Westminster, and pigeons at Hurlingham'. This is likely a reference to the fact that Parliament had been prorogued on 21 August and sessions would not resume again until November of that year. Shooting pigeons at Hurlingham was a relatively new pastime in 1871, with the Club only having been formed in 1869. It had begun as the Gun Club in 1860, founded by the sportsman, Frank Heathcote, at Hornsey Wood House, a popular site for shooting amongst the aristocracy. In 1867, with the establishment of Finsbury Park, members of the Gun Club needed to find a new home and approached Richard Naylor, owner of Hurlingham House in Fulham, to request permission to promote pigeon shooting at the estate. A license was granted and the first competition was held there in 1868. The following year, the estate was leased from Naylor and the Hurlingham Club was formed. Though pigeon shooting at Hurlingham would fall out of fashion, the pigeon remains on the club's logo to this day.

1
THE REAL 'AUTUMN SESSION'
MR PUNCH (TO THE EARL OF
WHATSITSNAME, AND THE RIGHT
HONOURABLE ALGERNON SCRUBBINGBRUSH, M.P.):
'AHA, MY NOBLE AND RIGHT HONOURABLE FRIENDS!
THIS IS BETTER THAN MURDERING BILLS
AT WESTMINSTER, AND PIGEONS AT
HURLINGHAM, EH?'
Signed with monogram
Pencil drawing of Mr Punch and a
figure on reverse
Pencil
8 ¼ × 6 ¼ INCHES
Illustrated: *Punch*, 2 September 1871, page 93

2

THE DEMON 'ROUGH'

JUSTICE: 'LOOK HERE, YOU COWARDLY RUFFIAN! THIS HAS
PUT DOWN GAROTTERS! WE SHALL NOW HAVE TO TRY IF
IT WON'T PUT DOWN YOU!'
Signed with monogram
Pencil
8 ¼ × 6 ¼ INCHES
Illustrated: *Punch*, 3 October 1874, page 140

THE DEMON 'ROUGH'

On 18 May 1874, Conservative politician Egerton Leigh spoke
in the House of Commons about the rise in domestic violence
against women and that a likely factor was the insufficient
punishment inflicted upon offenders. Leigh pointed out that
men were often not prosecuted at all, and if they were, the
sentence of six months' imprisonment or a fine, was not
sufficient to stop the rise in violence. He proposed to give the
Court a power to order flogging with the cat o' nine tails when
it deemed it necessary, of adding to the number of lashes on the
repetition of the offence, and, finally, of penal servitude. Whilst
acknowledging the seriousness of the issue, the Prime Minister
Benjamin Disraeli effectively shelved the issue by reassuring the
House that they would attend to the matter when time allowed,
but would not be able to address it immediately.

Egerton Leigh had argued that the use of the cat o' nine tails,
the multi-tailed whip that had traditionally been used as
punishment in the Navy, had successfully curbed the threat of
garrotting in London through its use in gaols. During the 1850s
and 60s, a number of moral panics had swept through London
over the rise in violent street muggings. Particularly feared was
garrotting, where a mugger would approach their victim from
behind and subdue them with a cord or an arm around their
neck while an accomplice robbed them of their valuables. The
press blamed the leniency of punishment on this rise in crime,
particularly after the cessation of transportation to Australia.
The fear of being garrotted sometimes resulted in members of
the public wearing anti-garrotting clothing, such as studded
leather collars and cravats with razor blades sewn in, a move
which was parodied at the time by *Punch*. In July 1863, the
Security from Violence Act, which specifically targeted street
robbery and become known informally as the Garrotters Act,
was passed. The act undid reforms that had abolished flogging
for most offences, allowing garrotters to be flogged in prison
for their crime.

A cartoon by John Tenniel on the subject had first appeared in
Punch on 30 May 1874. The present cartoon, published a little
over four months later, suggests the matter of violence against
women was a subject of debate amongst many.

THE JUBILEE 'MEET'

On 20 and 21 June 1887, Queen Victoria celebrated her Golden Jubilee, marking the 50th anniversary of her accession to the throne on 20 June 1837. In this cartoon published on 1 January 1887, Mr Punch welcomes in the new year in the form of a veteran huntsman at the 'Jubilee Meet'.

3
THE JUBILEE 'MEET'
THE OLD HUNTSMAN: 'YOU STICK TO ME, YOUNG SIR. I'LL SHOW YOU THE WAY!!'
Signed with monogram and dated 1887
Pencil
8 × 6 ¼ INCHES
Illustrated: *Punch*, 1 January 1887, page 7

HOW ABOUT THE DONKEY?

ISMAIL. "GET OFF!" BISMILLAH! WHO'S TO GET ON? ALL THESE FRANKS—OR SON TEWFIK, WITH THE PADISHAH BEHIND HIM? PLEASANT LOOK-OUT FOR THE DONKEY, EITHER WAY!"

"The Sultan's firman has arrived at Alexandria, pronouncing the deposition of the Khedive, and the nomination of Prince Tewfik in his stead." —Reuter's Eastern Telegram.

The cartoon as it appeared in *Punch* in 1879

4 *(opposite)*

HOW ABOUT THE DONKEY?
ISMAIL: '"GET OFF!" BISMILLAH!
WHO'S TO GET ON? ALL THESE FRANKS —
OR SON TEWFIK, WITH THE PADISHAH
BEHIND HIM? PLEASANT LOOK-OUT FOR
THE DONKEY, EITHER WAY!'
'THE SULTAN'S FIRMAN HAS ARRIVED AT
ALEXANDRIA, PRONOUNCING THE
DEPOSITION OF KHEDIVE, AND THE
NOMINATION OF PRINCE TEWFIK IN
HIS STEAD.' —
REUTER'S EASTERN TELEGRAM
Signed with monogram
Pencil
6 ¼ × 8 ¼ INCHES
Illustrated: *Punch*, 5 July 1879, page 307

HOW ABOUT THE DONKEY?

On 26 June 1879, a firman, or Royal mandate, from the Sultan of the Ottoman Empire, Abdul Hamid II, ordered the deposition of the Khedive of Egypt, Ismail Pasha. He was replaced as ruler by his eldest son, Tewfik Pasha, though the country was effectively in control of British and French financial ministers. After becoming Khedive (or Viceroy) of Egypt and Sudan in 1863, Ismail had run up deep debts to the Western Powers through extravagant borrowing to finance internal reforms, the building of the Suez Canal and, between 1874 and 1876, an expensive war with Ethiopia. In 1876, a British and French report into the state of the Egyptian finances resulted in the establishment of the 'Caisse de la Dette', an international commission to supervise the payment of the loans to the European governments. Further investigations led to the establishment of Anglo-French control over finances and the government. Such a degree of European interference was seen as unacceptable to many

Egyptians, who began to unite behind an Egyptian Colonel, Ahmed 'Urabi, in what became known as the 'Urabi Revolt. In response to Ismail's part reluctance and part inability to restore order and control, the British and French governments pressed for his removal and replacement by the more pliable Tewfik.

Published a week after Ismail's removal, he is portrayed in the present cartoon as receiving his deposition whilst astride a donkey representing Egypt. He is shown questioning who exactly may be replacing him, whether it is his son, Tewfik, with the Padishah (the Ottman Sultan) behind him, or if it is in fact the 'Franks' or Western Powers. The Powers are represented here by Lord Salisbury, the British Foreign Secretary, the German Chancellor Otto von Bismarck, and the Italian Prime Minister Benedetto Cairoli.

The cartoon as it appeared in *Punch* in 1889

SUGAR!

In April 1888, an International Conference was held in London to discuss the question of sugar bounties, attended by all the bounty-giving powers. The object of the Conference for the British government was to endeavour to mutually agree on the best means of the abolition of these sugar bounties. Pictured here feeding the young John Bull a spoonful of sugar is the President of the Conference and the British Plenipotentiary, Henry de Worms, Conservative politician and Under-Secretary of State for the Colonies. At this time, much of Britain's sugar was produced and supplied by its colonies, whereas the majority of sugar distributed on the continent was produced from beet sugar in European countries such as Germany. The result of the Conference was the signature of a Convention by the representatives of Great Britain and the bounty-giving Powers, which contained a penal clause by which the signatories agreed to exclude bounty-fed sugar, either by absolute prohibition or by counter-vailing duties levied upon it. A year later however and this agreement had not yet come into effect and the continuing bounties on sugar production on the continent was seen as a threat to sugar export and production in Britain and its colonies.
This cartoon published in *Punch* in May 1889 suggests a fear amongst the British public that a rising cost of sugar may force sugar producers to add other substances to their sugar in order to keep up with demand.

5 (opposite)
SUGAR!
DR DE WORMS. 'NOW THEN MASTER JOHNNIE, OPEN YOUR MOUTH AND SHUT YOUR EYES, HERE'S A NICE SPOONFUL OF SUGAR FOR YOU!'
JOHNNIE BULL (SUSPICIOUSLY). 'BUT, I SAY! – IS IT ALL SUGAR?'
Signed with monogram
Pencil
8 × 6 ¼ INCHES
Illustrated: *Punch*, 11 May 1889, page 227
Literature: *Sir John Tenniel's Cartoons From Punch 1882-1891*, London: Bradbury, Agnew & Co, 1895

COUNTRY AND DUTY

Published during the Whitsun Recess of Parliament (23 May to 2 June 1890), the present cartoon features William Henry Smith (1825-1891), son of the founder of the newsagent and booksellers W H Smith, and the First Lord of the Treasury and Leader of the House of Commons under Lord Salisbury's Conservative government. The cartoon was published in *Punch* alongside a satirical song entitled 'Country and Duty', sung by 'Old Morality', the nickname given to Smith by the *Punch* writer H W Lucy and by which he became widely known on account of his conscientious and austere manner. In the song, W H Smith revels in the peace and quiet afforded to him by the break in Parliamentary proceedings and that he will be ready to muzzle the 'yelping and yapping' and 'howling and whining' of his colleagues in the Commons. In the cartoon, he polishes a rusty muzzle in preparation for the return of Parliament.

It was acknowledged at the time that W H Smith led the house when the management of the Commons was particularly difficult, with a number of strong-willed and hot-headed figures at the fore. The strains of the role eventually became too great and he retired from public life less than a year after the publication of the present cartoon due to ill health, dying a few months later on 6 October 1891 of heart failure.

The cartoon as it appeared in *Punch* in 1890

6
COUNTRY AND DUTY
MR W H S: 'IT'S GOT A LITTLE RUSTY, —
BUT I'LL HAVE IT READY IN TIME!'
Signed with monogram
Pencil
8 ¼ × 6 ¼ INCHES
Illustrated: *Punch*, 31 May 1890, page 259

7
ON THE PROWL
Signed with monogram
Pencil
6 × 8 INCHES
Illustrated: *Punch*, 28 August 1886

ON THE PROWL

Throughout much of the nineteenth century, diplomatic and political relations between the British and Russian Empires had grown increasingly tense over each side's respective interests in Central Asia, in what became known as the 'Great Game'. In 1828, Russian victory in the Russo-Persian War had seen Armenia become part of the Russian Empire, and following the accession of Tsar Alexander II in 1855, Russia had begun an aggressive expansionist policy to the south and the east, primarily to obtain naval access to the Black Sea. British mistrust of Russian foreign policy in the region was borne out of a fear that Russia would eventually push south through Afghanistan and threaten British interests in India. The signing of the Treaty of San Stefano in March 1878 between Russia and the Ottoman Empire, following Russian victory in the Russo-Turkish War of 1877-1878, created a larger, independent Bulgaria under Russian protection, further strengthening Russian influence in the region.

In 1881, British concerns were heightened further when Russian troops occupied Turkmen lands on the Persian and Afghan borders. Only a diplomatic intervention by Germany prevented an Anglo-Russian war.

In 1885, tensions almost came to a head when Russian forces engaged with and captured an Afghan border fort, in what became known as the Panjdeh Incident. Britain viewed this attack against a British protectorate as a precursor to an imminent invasion of India and prepared for war. However both sides were able to defuse the crisis diplomatically, and the signing of the Delimitation Protocol between Britain and Russia in September 1885 defined the north-western border of Afghanistan and ended Russian expansion in the region. Almost a year later however, John Tenniel's cartoon of a Russian bear moving through the Balkans towards Afghanistan, suggests that the British still mistrusted Russian intentions in the region.

CHARLES KEENE
Charles Samuel Keene (1823-1891)

Associated, from the 1860s, with his *Punch* cartoons of urban street life, Charles Keene developed a great reputation as a draughtsman, and was revered by many of his contemporaries.

Charles Keene was born in Duvals Lane, Hornsey, Middlesex, on 10 August 1823, one of the sons of the solicitor, Samuel Keene, and his wife, Mary (née Sparrow). He spent his childhood in London and Ipswich, where he was educated at the local grammar school. He then spent some time in the offices of both his late father, at Furnivall's Inn, London, and the architect, William Pilkington of Scotland Yard. However, finding neither congenial, he entered a five-year apprenticeship with the wood-engravers, the Whymper Brothers. In addition, he was 'a compulsive attender' of the Clipstone Academy, from 1848 into the 1860s.

Keene illustrated books from 1847 and contributed to *The Illustrated London News*, but it was only in December 1851, when he made his first, unsigned drawing for *Punch*, that he found the ideal outlet for his talents. It was a connection that lasted until the day of his death and, from the time he began to use his monogram in 1854, it brought him great celebrity. Keene became a member of the *Punch* 'Table' in 1860 and, on the death of John Leech in 1864, took on the role of chief social commentator. He relied principally on urban street life, thus complementing the drawings of George Du Maurier, who was employed from the same year. He greatly inspired Phil May, who was in some ways his successor, but Keene was less intrinsically funny and made much use of comic situations supplied by his friend Joseph Crawhall senior. His influence lay for the most part in the areas of style and technique and, as an admirer and correspondent of Adolf Menzel, he did much to introduce the German tradition of draughtsmanship into Britain. Praised by the French, and working late in life in a style reminiscent of Toulouse-Lautrec, he has been described with some justification as 'the English Daumier' (Gordon Ray, *The Illustrator and the Book in England from 1790 to 1914*, New York: Pierrepoint Morgan Library, 1976, page 118). Whistler went further and called him 'the greatest English artist since Hogarth' (quoted in Joseph Pennell, *Pen Drawing and Pen Draughtsmen*, New York: Macmillan, 1920, page 236).

Through most of his career, Keene lived 'in various dilapidated rooms and lodgings' in London (Houfe, *ODNB*). However, he also took a cottage in Witley, Surrey, for some years, and spent long holidays in Suffolk. Two months after his death on 4 January 1891, at his final home at 112 Hammersmith Road, London, the Fine Art Society mounted a memorial exhibition.

His work is represented in numerous public collections, including the British Museum, the National Portrait Gallery, Tate and the V&A; the Ashmolean Museum (Oxford) and The Fitzwilliam Museum (Cambridge).

Further reading:
Simon Houfe, *Charles Keene. 'the Artist's Artist' 1823-1891*, London: Christie's/Punch, 1991;
Simon Houfe, 'Keene, Charles Samuel (1823-1891)', H C G Matthew and Brian Harrison (eds), *Oxford Dictionary of National Biography*, Oxford University Press, 2004, vol 31, pages 29-32;
Simon Houfe, *The Work of Charles Samuel Keene*, London: Scolar Press, 1995;
Derek Hudson, *Charles Keene*, London: Pleiades Books, 1947;
Lewis Johnson, 'Keene, Charles (Samuel) (*b* London, 10 Aug 1823; *d* London, 4 Jan 1891)', Jane Turner (ed), *The Dictionary of Art*, London: Macmillan, 1996, vol 17, page 877

8
BEWILDERING
MR WUZZLES (UP FOR THE CATTLE SHOW): 'CHEESE, WAITER!'
ROBERT. 'YESSIR! ROCKFOR, COMMONBARE, GREW'ERE, NOOCHATTELL, GORGUMZO – '
MR WUZZLES (TESTILY): 'NO, NO! I SAID CHEESE!'
Ink
4 ¾ × 4 INCHES
Illustrated: *Punch*, 16 December 1882, page 281

9

PUT TO THE ROUT

DISTRACTED BANDSTER: 'KOMM AVAY – KOMM AVAY – EE ZHALL NOD GIVE YOU NODINGSH –
EE VILL BLAY DE MOOZEEK ERSELBST! TEUFEL!

[THEY RETREAT HASTILY.]

Signed with initials

Ink

4 ¼ × 6 ¾ INCHES

Illustrated: *Punch*, 13 July 1878, page 6

Literature: *The Strand Magazine*, 1899, page 40;

J Holt Schooling, *A Peep Into 'Punch'*, London: George Newnes, 1900;

J A Hamerton (ed), *Book of Mr Punch's Scottish Humour*, London: Educational Book Company, 1910

10

GENERALLY APPLICABLE; A SCENE IN AN IRISH LAND COURT

SUB COMMISSIONER: 'NOW MURPHY, HAVE YOU EFFECTED ANY IMPROVEMENT IN THIS FARM'

TENANT: 'I HAVE, YER HONOUR. IVER SINCE I GOT IT, I'VE BEEN IMPROVIN IT. BUT BY JABERS, IT'S THAT SORT O' LAND THE MORE YE IMPROVE IT THE WORSE IT GETS'

COURT REDUCES THE RENT 25 PER CENT

Signed with initials and bears collector's stamp 'GE'

Ink

6 ½ × 9 ½ INCHES

Illustrated: *Punch*, 28 March 1885, page 146

11

A MISCONCEPTION

PASSENGER: 'AND WHOSE HOUSE IS THAT ON THE TOP OF THE HILL THERE?'

DRIVER OF THE 'RED LION' BUS: 'O, THAT'S MR UMBERBROWN'S, SIR. HE'S WHAT THEY CALL A R.A.'

PASSENGER (AMATEUR ARTIST): 'O, INDEED! AH! A MAGNIFICENT PAINTER! YOU MUST BE RATHER PROUD OF SUCH A GREAT MAN LIVING AMONGST YOU DOWN HERE!'

DRIVER: 'GREAT MAN, SIR? LOR 'BLESS YER, SIR, NOT A BIT OF IT! WHY, THEY ONLY KEEPS ONE MAN SERVANT, AND HE DON'T SLEEP IN THE 'OUSE!!!'

Stamped with monogram
Ink
4 ¼ × 6 ¾ INCHES
Illustrated: *Punch*, 20 January 1872, page 32

12

OUR RESERVES

COLONEL OF VOLUNTEERS (HAVING CLUBBED THE BATTALION SEVERAL TIMES DURING THE DRILL)

'HAS Y'WERE! - 'ALT! - MARK TIME! THE 'OLE WILL BEAR IN MIND THAT MY WORD O' COMMAND IS MERELY "A CAUTION"!'

[A REMARK WITH WHICH THE 'OLE OF THE REGIMENT ENTIRELY AGREED]

Signed with monogram
Ink with bodycolour
7 × 10 ¼ INCHES
Provenance: Luke Gertler
Illustrated: *Punch*, 3 August 1878, page 42

GEORGE DU MAURIER

George Louis Palmella Busson Du Maurier (1834-1896)

Equally talented as artist and writer, George Du Maurier developed a cartoon format for *Punch* that balanced text and image in order to record and satirise the fashions and foibles of society.

The eldest of the three children of the scientist and inventor, Louis-Mathurin Du Maurier, and his wife, Ellen (née Clarke), George Du Maurier was born on 6 March 1834 in the Champs-Elysées, Paris, and baptised in May 1835 at Rotherfield, Sussex. He spent his childhood, between England and the continent, in an atmosphere of precarious gentility. His father came from a French family of master glassblowers but, obsessed with social status, gave himself the aristocratic name of Du Maurier. As a novelist, George Du Maurier would rehearse the events of his early life in general but, as a cartoonist for *Punch*, he would concentrate on dissecting the pretensions and foibles of the society in which he lived, and to which his family had been prey.

Though Du Maurier failed his *baccalauréat*, his father was determined that he should take up a steady profession. So, in 1851, he enrolled at the Birkbeck Chemical Laboratory, University College, London. After a wasted year, he left to work as an analytical chemist, but spent his most profitable hours drawing at the British Museum so that, on the death of his father in 1856, he returned to Paris to study art. He spent a sociable year at the Atelier Gleyre as part of the English group, befriending Edward Poynter and meeting James McNeill Whistler, and then moved to Antwerp to further his studies at the city's Academy of Arts, under Jacob Van Lerius. The sudden loss of the sight of his left eye, however, led to a period of great uncertainty as to his future career. Joined by his mother, he lived first at Malines and later at Düsseldorf, desperately consulting oculists while still attempting to work. In 1860, he finally decided to settle in London and, encouraged by the example of John Leech, tried to earn his living as an illustrator.

In London, Du Maurier reacquainted himself with Whistler and members of the English group, and became immersed in an enlightened social circle while beginning to contribute – as artist and writer – to such leading periodicals as, *Good Words* and *The Cornhill Magazine*. By evolving his own style from the work of the finest of contemporary illustrators, he developed the extensive repertoire of immediately recognisable motifs and gestures on which he drew increasingly for the satires and parodies that he published in *Punch*.

In 1863, Du Maurier married Emma Wightwick, and they would have five children, the youngest of whom, Gerald, became famous as an actor-manager. From 1869, he and his family lived in Hampstead, settling at 27 Church Row in 1870, and moving to New Grove House in 1874.

Du Maurier became a regular member of the *Punch* team in 1864, when John Tenniel and Charles Keene both voted for him to succeed the recently deceased Leech as observer of society. In its pages he developed a very literary type of cartoon, which married often extensive texts to subtle drawing and displayed an understanding of wider cultural issues. This reached its peak in his satires of the upper middle class attempting to follow the fashions of the Aesthetic Movement. Through his career, he moved from a position of Bohemianism – from which he defended the Pre-Raphaelites and tolerated Whistler – to one that, at worst, revealed 'his essential snobbery, conservatism and loathing of change' (Ormond, 1969, page 248), and inevitably lost him many friends.

Du Maurier has been dubbed as 'naturally lazy' (by Simon Houfe in *The Dictionary of 19th Century British Book Illustrators and Caricaturists*, Woodbridge: Antique Collectors' Club, 1996, page 124). However, he had to provide for his wife and children without straining his one good eye. For much of his career, he could work safely for only two hours a day, and during the 1890s considered retiring from illustration in order to become a professional lecturer. By that time, he needed to work with a magnifying glass in order to complete his regular work for *Punch*.

But as his graphic talent failed, he found new, and phenomenal, success as the novelist of *Peter Ibbetson* (1891), *The Martian* (1896) and particularly *Trilby* (1894), in which he returned to the youthful extremes of Bohemian life that he had eschewed in his cartoons. He died on 8 October 1896 at 17 Oxford Square, Paddington, his home from 1895. A memorial show was held at the Fine Art Society in February 1897.

His work is represented in numerous public collections, including the British Museum and the V&A.

Further reading:

Leonée Ormond, 'Du Maurier, George Louis Palmella Busson (1834-1896)', in H C G Matthew and Brian Harrison (eds), *Oxford Dictionary of National Biography*, Oxford University Press, 2004, volume 17, pages 177-180;
Leonée Ormond, *George Du Maurier*, London: Routledge & Kegan Paul, 1969;
Leonée Ormond, 'Du Maurier, George (Louis Palmella Busson) (*b* Paris, 6 March 1834; *d* London, 8 Oct 1896)', in Jane Turner (ed), *The Dictionary of Art*, London: Macmillan, 1996, vol 9, page 384

13

THE CHILD OF THE PERIOD

NEW GOVERNESS: 'WHY ARE YOU TEARING THAT PLACARD, ELSIE?
I THOUGHT YOUR PAPA WAS A LIBERAL!'

ELSIE: 'SO HE IS — AND THE ONLY ONE IN THE FAMILY'

Signed

Signed, inscribed with title and dated 'Nov 1885' on text label

Ink

4 ¾ x 7 ½ INCHES

Illustrated: *Punch*, 12 December 1885, page 282

Exhibited: The Fine Art Society, London, 1887, no 80;

The Fine Art Society, London, July 2001

14
THE DU MAURIER FAMILY IN CORNWALL
Signed
Ink
6 ½ x 9 ¼ INCHES

15

SYMPATHETIC EGOISM OF GENIUS (A STUDY)

'DON'T RUN AWAY YET, OLD MAN! IT'S QUITE EARLY, AND I WANT TO HEAR ALL ABOUT YOUR ACADEMY PICTURE, WHICH I'M TOLD IS SPLENDID.'

[PROCEEDS TO DESCRIBE HIS OWN AT GREAT LENGTH, AND THEN SUDDENLY FINDS OUT HOW LATE IT IS, AND BOLTS...]

Signed, inscribed with title and dated 'Jan 91'

Ink; 9 × 6 ¼ INCHES

Illustrated: *Punch*, 7 February 1891, page 71

16

THEORY AND PRACTICES

AUNT MARY: 'WHY DON'T YOU READ, TOM, INSTEAD OF LOLLING ABOUT'

TOM: 'GOT NOTHING TO READ!'

AUNT MARY: 'THERE'S YOUR FIRST PRIZE IN MONSIEUR JOLIVET'S FRENCH CLASS, A MOST DELIGHTFUL BOOK!'

TOM: 'HOW CAN I READ THAT? IT'S IN FRENCH!'

Signed

Signed, inscribed with title and 'Punch', and dated 'Feb 3 1877' on mount

Ink; 5 ¼ × 8 ½ INCHES

Illustrated: *Punch*, 3 February 1877, page 42

Victorian Illustrators
& Cartoonists

VICTORIAN ILLUSTRATORS & CARTOONISTS

KATE GREENAWAY
Kate Greenaway RI (1846-1901)

The characteristic charm of Kate Greenaway's illustrations resides in a simplicity of both vision and visual style. A past time – the Regency – is represented through clear outline and flat wash as the embodiment of innocence; an eternal English spring is peopled, for the most part, by graceful youths engaged in gentle occupation.

Kate Greenaway was born in Hoxton, East London, on 17 March 1846. The urban background of her childhood gave her a longing for the countryside, a longing made more definite and painful by happy memories of family holidays in Nottinghamshire. She would transform these desires into the enchanted yet homely visual world that made her name.

The favourite daughter of a wood-engraver to *The Illustrated London News*, Greenaway studied at the Finsbury School of Art, the National Art Training School, South Kensington, and, in 1870-71, at the Heatherley School of Fine Art. In 1871, she enrolled at the Slade School of Art, and spent time in the life class of the director, Edward Poynter, there meeting Helen Allingham, who later became a close friend. Greenaway's earliest fairy illustrations were robust, painterly and even grotesque, so revealing the influence of her distant cousin, Richard Dadd. But the child portraits that she exhibited at the Royal Academy, from 1877, more clearly marked the direction of her developing career. In the same year, she began to work for the printer and publisher Edmund Evans, who recognised her original ability to emphasise the innocence of childhood through the use of a Regency setting. Her illustrated books and various designs – epitomised by *The Kate Greenaway Almanack* (which appeared between 1888 and 1897) – soon became enormously popular in both Britain and the United States. And, with Ruskin acting as champion and adviser, her fame and stature rapidly increased. She was elected to the membership of the Royal Institute of Painters in Water Colours (RI) in 1889, and held three solo shows at the Fine Art Society (1891, 1893 and 1897). A fourth, memorial show was held at the gallery in the year following her death at Hampstead on 6 November 1901.

Her work is represented in the collections of the British Museum and the V&A; and the Ashmolean Museum (Oxford) and Manchester Art Gallery.

17

STUDY OF A YOUNG GIRL WITH A FEATHERED BONNET, CREAM SKIRT AND BROWN JACKET
Signed with initials
Watercolour
3 ½ x 3 ½ inches
Provenance: Brown & Phillips, Leicester Galleries, London

Further Reading:
Rodney Engen, *Kate Greenaway: A Biography*, London: Macdonald, 1981;
Rosemary Mitchell, 'Greenaway, Catherine [Kate] (1846-1901)', H C G Matthew and Brian Harrison (eds), *Oxford Dictionary of National Biography*, Oxford University Press, 2004, vol 23, pages 549-553; Emma M Routh, 'Greenaway, Kate (*b* Hoxton, London, 17 March 1846; *d* Hampstead, London, 6 Nov 1901), Jane Turner (ed), *The Dictionary of Art*, London: Macmillan, 1996, vol 13, page 615;
M H Spielmann and G S Layard, *Kate Greenaway*, London: Adam and Charles Black, 1905

18
MAY BLOSSOM
Watercolour
9 ½ x 7 ½ INCHES

19
LITTLE GIRL WITH MUFF
Signed with initials
Watercolour
10 ½ x 7 ½ INCHES
Provenance: Stark Museum of Art, Texas

PHIL MAY
Philip William May, RI RP NEAC (1864-1903)

Sometimes referred to as the 'grandfather of British illustration', Phil May was one of the most influential black-and-white artists of his generation. Earthy, street-wise, and redolent of the music hall, his work is the antithesis of that of Aubrey Beardsley.

For a biography of Phil May, please refer to *The Illustrators*, 2017, page 36.

21
LITTLE SNOOKS (TO CELEBRATED ACTRESS JUST RETURNED FROM AMERICA): 'AWFULLY GLAD TO SEE YOU'RE BACK AGAIN, MISS DE VERE'
Signed
Inscribed with title and stamped with M W Ingram collection mark below mount
Ink; 10 × 6 ¾ INCHES
Provenance: M W Ingram

20
AT THE RACES
Signed and dated 95
Inscribed 'John Porter' and 'Lord Allington' below mount
Ink
10 ¼ × 6 ¾ INCHES

22 *(opposite)*
GROUP OF CHILDREN WAITING FOR A FREE DINNER
Signed, inscribed with title and dated 95
Signed and dated 95 on original mount
Pencil
9 ¼ × 11 ¾ INCHES

23
RAMSGATE SANDS
Signed twice, inscribed 'To Lear J Drew from his friend' and 'Ramsgate', and dated 97
Ink with pencil
7 ½ x 11 ¼ INCHES
Provenance: Lear J Drew;
Hugh Blaker;
Cyril Kenneth Bird, known as 'Fougasse', purchased from the Leicester Galleries, 1948
Exhibited: 'From the Hugh Blaker Collection', Leicester Galleries, London, March 1948, no 5

E J SULLIVAN
Edmund Joseph Sullivan, RWS RE IS (1869-1933)

E J Sullivan was one of the most striking and confident illustrators of his generation, ranging across many moods and media, and becoming a particularly influential teacher.

For a biography of Edmund Joseph Sullivan, please refer to *The Illustrators*, 2016, pages 6-7.

Published in late 1915, *The Kaiser's Garland* was a collection of 45 cartoons by E J Sullivan satirising the German Emperor, Kaiser Wilhelm, and criticising the barbarism and brutality of Prussian militarism.

24
THE KAISER'S GARLAND
Signed with initials
Ink
11 ½ × 17 ½ INCHES
Illustrated: Edmund J Sullivan, *The Kaiser's Garland*,
London: William Heinemann, 1915, cover

25
DIABLE, ET MA GAUCHE!
Inscribed with title on reverse
Ink
10 ¼ × 7 ¼ INCHES
Drawn for but not illustrated in: Edmund J Sullivan, *The Kaiser's Garland*,
London: William Heinemann, 1915

26
MARCHING SKELETONS
Ink
10 ¼ x 7 INCHES
Illustrated: Edmund J Sullivan,
The Kaiser's Garland, London:
William Heinemann, 1915, page 63

27
PRIMA BALLERINA ASSOLUTA TO THE IMPERIAL BALLET
OF POTSDAM IN HER NOTED FIRE AND SWORD DANCE
Signed and dated 1915
Ink
10 ½ x 7 ¼ INCHES
Illustrated: Edmund J Sullivan, *The Kaiser's Garland*, London:
William Heinemann, 1915, page 25

28
THE PRISONER OF WAR
Ink
10 ½ x 7 ¼ INCHES
Illustrated: Edmund J Sullivan, *The Kaiser's Garland*,
London: William Heinemann, 1915, page 69

29
MORE COLD THAN DEATH
Signed and dated 1915
Ink
10 ½ × 7 ¼ INCHES
Illustrated: Edmund J Sullivan, *The Kaiser's Garland*,
London: William Heinemann, 1915, page 81

30
THE WRITING ON THE WALL
'GOD HATH NUMBERED THY KINGDOM AND FINISHED IT. THOU ART WEIGHED
IN THE BALANCES AND ART FOUND WANTING. THY KINGDOM IS DIVIDED AND
GIVEN TO THE MEDES AND PERSIANS.' - DANIEL V. 26-28
Signed and dated 1915
Ink
10 × 7 INCHES
Illustrated: Edmund J Sullivan, *The Kaiser's Garland*, London:
William Heinemann, 1915, page 85

Vanity Fair

VANITY FAIR

*'I venture to prophesy that, when the history of the Victorian
Era comes to be written in true perspective, the most faithful mirror
and record of representative men and the spirit of their
times will be sought and found in* Vanity Fair'
(Leslie Ward, *Forty Years of 'Spy'*, page 331)

When, on 7 November 1868, the first edition of the new 'society journal' *Vanity Fair* was published, there was little indication within its pages of the influence it was to have on Victorian high society. This first edition contained no caricatures, its text commented on the week's social and political events and reviewed the latest literary and theatrical releases. The journal failed to find immediate success and struggled to compete with other more established papers such as *The Owl* and *The Tomahawk*. *Vanity Fair's* founder, Thomas Gibson Bowles, was the son of a prominent liberal politician, Thomas Milner Gibson, and his wife, Susannah Arethusa Gibson, who was well established in influential social circles and regularly hosted fashionable salons. Growing up within this environment, Bowles was able to socialise with journalists, actors, artists, politicians and bohemians. Whilst maintaining a junior position at the Board of Trade, he began to contribute to various journals, including *The Glow Worm*, *The Owl* and *The Tomahawk*. Though it was his experiences with these publications that gave Bowles the confidence to create his own journal, it was his social connections that not only helped it get off the ground, but also shaped its future. A close friend, Colonel Frederick Gustavus Burnaby, supplied £100 of the £200 original investment and, although Bowles wrote much of the text himself under the pseudonym 'Jehu Junior', he engaged regular contributors to participate. These contributors were selected from fashionable sets for their social as much as their literary qualifications. Indeed, *Vanity Fair* was written by and for the Victorian and Edwardian establishment.

On 16 January 1869, Bowles promised his readers 'Some Pictorial Wares of an entirely novel character'. What was to follow not only set *Vanity Fair* apart from its competitors, but changed the way in which caricature was viewed and received. Two weeks later, a full-page caricature of Benjamin Disraeli by Carlo Pellegrini appeared in *Vanity Fair*, followed the next week by a caricature of William Gladstone. The images were reproduced by the highly regarded lithographer, Vincent Brooks, using an approach that was virtually unprecedented in England. Until this point, lithography had been reserved largely for topographical and decorative subjects. Cartoons and caricatures, such as those published in popular satirical magazines like *Punch*, were reproduced through wood-engraving. Pellegrini's caricatures, completed under the pseudonym 'Singe' (later 'Ape') were the first of over 2,300 caricatures to be published in *Vanity Fair*. These highly-skilled, lithographically reproduced, full-page cartoons, in a journal published in quarto dimensions with 8-10 pages per issue, gave *Vanity Fair* an instant identity.

Carlo Pellegrini collaborated with Thomas Gibson Bowles and Vincent Brooks with enormous success. A favourite of the Prince of Wales, the immensely popular Neapolitan mixed easily with his subjects and portrayed them gently, making it something of a mark of honour, even a social necessity, to appear in *Vanity Fair's* pages. Before then, the nature of English caricature had been shaped by the savage work of the Georgian cartoonists such as Thomas Rowlandson and James Gillray. Pellegrini diluted the ferocity of these cartoons through his own style, influenced by his early years caricaturing bohemian society in Naples, and by the work of his fellow Neapolitan, Melchiorre Delfico (who would later contribute eight drawings to *Vanity Fair*). The gently humorous style of caricature that was introduced to England by the likes of Pellegrini and Delfico was immediately more palatable to the sensibilities of Victorian Society than the more brutal satire made popular in France.

The success of Carlo Pellegrini and the burgeoning popularity of *Vanity Fair* made the magazine an attractive proposition for foreign artists seeking patronage in the upper echelons of society. In 1869, the French society painter, James Tissot began to contribute under the pseudonym 'Coïdé', bringing a more serious, portraiture style to the magazine. This suited the preferences of Thomas Bowles Gibson, but, understanding that Pellegrini's more satirical drawings were what had brought him success, sought other more humorous collaborators to work alongside him. These included Adriano Cecioni, Melchiorre Delfico, Francis Carruthers Gould and the American political cartoonist, Thomas Nast.

The arrival of Leslie Ward at *Vanity Fair* in 1873 turned the magazine into a national institution. Drawing under the pseudonym 'Spy', Ward was industrious, dependable and passionate. Bowles Gibson came to depend on him over the mercurial Pellegrini, who left *Vanity Fair* on a number of occasions to pursue other ventures. For 40 years, 'Spy' caricatured the highest profile figures in Victorian society, from actors and sportsmen to politicians and royalty. Having grown up rubbing shoulders with those whom he now caricatured, through his family connections and personal acquaintances, he was able to move easily in these social circles. He considered himself no bohemian, rather he saw himself as a professional, dedicated to his craft. To be caricatured by 'Spy' and for the result to appear in *Vanity Fair* was a confirmation of one's importance to Victorian society.

Though Leslie Ward's approach to his art changed the perception of caricature in Victorian England, it was not always for the better. In *Vanity Fair's* early days, this respectable, often flattering form of caricature was something entirely new. In the light of this novelty, it was viewed in the right spirit by those portrayed. Later, as Ward lamented in his autobiography, *Forty Years of Spy*, those he drew began to grow particular and demanding about how they were represented. Ward began his career at *Vanity Fair* physically seeking out his subjects around London; as he grew busier, he began to request that many came to sit for him at his studio. Frequently, he received sitters who would pay for the privilege of being caricatured. This opened an entirely new form of subject to him, and with it came a more commercial relationship between Ward and his sitters.

Despite the ongoing success of *Vanity Fair*, the attentions of Thomas Gibson Bowles had begun to focus elsewhere by the 1880s, and he was content to leave most of the illustrations to Leslie Ward. He had become more involved in politics (he would become Conservative MP for King's Lynn in 1892) and had other newspaper interests including *The Lady*, which he founded in 1884. In 1889, he sold *Vanity Fair* for £20,000 and was replaced as editor by A G Witherby. Although this did not immediately alter the character of the magazine, the death of Pellegrini in January 1889 left Ward as the only experienced member of staff. For the next decade, the only other regular contributor of illustrations was the French caricaturist, Jean Baptiste Guth.

Though some have argued that *Vanity Fair* fell into a decline in the twentieth century, having lost some of its wit and irreverence, it remained a proving ground for aspiring young artists, the most notable being Max Beerbohm, who contributed nine drawings to the magazine in its later years. *Vanity Fair's* final caricature, of Joseph Chamberlain drawn by 'Astz', was published on 14 January 1914. The following month, it was absorbed by *Hearth and Home*.

Other periodicals founded during this period purported to be society papers, but none came close to matching *Vanity Fair*. This was undoubtedly due to the consistent quality of cartoons from the likes of Ward and Pellegrini. Ward described *Mayfair*, a paper he occasionally drew for, as 'the only Society journal that I can recall having succeeded in any way on the lines of *Vanity Fair*' [*Forty Years of 'Spy'*, page 337]. A comment published in *The Week*, a Canadian journal, on 3 April 1884, claimed that whilst it was virtually unknown outside of London, *Vanity Fair* 'owes the small place it holds in flunkeydom to the clever cartoons of public characters which appear each week'.

Though *Vanity Fair* was, like many other similar magazines, a purveyor of 'backstairs court and aristocratic tittle-tattle' (as described by *The Week*), Leslie Ward described *Vanity Fair* in his autobiography as the first magazine that could rightfully call itself a society journal. Through the acerbic wit of Thomas Gibson Bowles and other contributors, and through the caricatures of 'Spy', *Vanity Fair* became the essential representation of Victorian high society, a paper written by and for the Establishment.

Further Reading:

Roy T. Matthews, Peter Mellini, In *'Vanity Fair'*, Berkeley, CA: University of California Press, 1982;
Leslie Ward, *Forty Years of 'Spy'*, London: Chatto & Windus, 1915

APE

Carlo Pellegrini (1839-1889), known as 'Ape'

Alongside his colleague Leslie Ward (who took the pen name 'Spy'), Carlo Pellegrini defined the look of the Victorian society journal, *Vanity Fair*. Inspired by the work of Melchiorre Delifco and Honoré Daumier, his caricatures, produced under the pen name 'Ape', had an enduring effect on Victorian high society as a whole. So did Pellegrini himself, as the eccentric Neapolitan caricaturist became known as one of London society's most well-known and well-loved figures.

Carlo Pellegrini was born in Capua, Campania, Italy, on 25 March 1839, a descendent of the Sedili Capuani, an aristocratic landowning family. He was educated at the Collegio Barnabiti, then at the Sant' Antonio in Maddaloni, near Caserta. By the age of 20, he had already established himself as a highly popular figure in Neapolitan high society. He was eccentric and funny, kind-hearted and generous. He quickly earned himself many friends and patrons and delighted many of them by drawing caricatures for them, though he had no formal artistic training.

In the autumn of 1860, it is possible that the young Pellegrini joined the forces of Giuseppe Garibaldi and fought in the last battles against the Bourbons at the Volturno and at Capua. Although this assertion is the subject of debate, as are many of his anecdotes, according to his *Vanity Fair* colleague, Leslie Ward.

On 9 November 1892, Pellegrini met the Prince of Wales during a visit to Naples, and celebrated his coming-of-age with him. This encounter was significant to his future career, as two years later, when he arrived in London, he was quickly ensconced as a close friend and jester in the Prince's social circle. Why he left Italy is unclear, though he maintained to friends that it was a combination of unrequited love and the death of his sister. He claims that he initially endured poverty when he first arrived in London, including periods sleeping rough in Whitehall and Piccadilly, but his reputation and popularity in London's bohemian society rapidly grew.

As he had done in Naples, Pellegrini regularly drew caricatures for his friends and royal companions. These caricatures came to the attention of Thomas Gibson Bowles, who had recently founded the society paper, *Vanity Fair*. He commissioned Pellegrini to produce colour portraits of Benjamin Disraeli and William Gladstone. These portraits were reproduced by Vincent Brooks, then London's premier lithographer and appeared in *Vanity Fair* in January and February 1869 under the pseudonym 'Singe', the French for 'ape'. His drawings were an immediate success and he became a permanent member of staff at *Vanity Fair*, producing caricatures under his new pseudonym, 'Ape'.

In the 1870s, he met and struck up a friendship with Edgar Degas, and the two men produced portraits of one another, Pellegrini's inscribed 'a vous', and Degas' 'a lui'. Remaining as highly sociable in London as he had been in Naples, Pellegrini was a member of the Arts Club from 1874 to 1888, and a member of the Beefsteak Club, along with Leslie Ward. It was here that he first met James McNeill Whistler, who became a great influence on his work. Pellegrini had long aspired to become a portrait painter to the level of Whistler, and twice left *Vanity Fair*, first in 1871 and again in 1876, in an attempt to succeed in this field. However, his talents for caricature did not extend to portraiture and, after his work in this field was poorly received by critics, he returned to *Vanity Fair* early in 1877. Though he was debilitated in his final years by tuberculosis, he continued to produce cartoons for *Vanity Fair* until his death on 22 January 1889.

At barely five feet two inches tall, with a large head and very small feet, Carlo Pellegrini certainly made a huge impression on those he met. He flaunted his homosexuality, at a time when it was dangerous to do so and dressed eccentrically, though flawlessly. As Leslie Ward observed, 'he always wore white spats, and their whiteness was ever immaculate, for he rode everywhere, a fact which probably accounted for his bad health in later years. His boots, too, were the acme of perfection, and his nails were as long and pointed as those of a mandarin' [*Forty Years of Spy*, page 96]. His story-telling at London society gatherings was legendary, despite his struggles with the language. Ward recalled that when regaling his listeners with his stories, 'his English, which was ever poor, stumbles and tripped, for although he was rather too quick to recollect slang terms, his grammar remained appalling, but delightfully naive' [*Forty Years of Spy*, page 97]. Such was his popularity that when he was debilitated by tuberculosis, his fashionable friends raised the money for his care in a private hospital, settled all his debts, and provided the luxuries to which he was accustomed until his death. The Fine Art Society sold a proof from a destroyed plate of his much admired caricature of Whistler, with Whistler's signature, to pay for his gravestone in Kensal Green Roman Catholic cemetery, London.

His work is represented in the collections of the National Portrait Gallery; and the Royal Library, Windsor.

Further reading:

Maria Cristina Chiusa, 'Pellegrini, Carlo *(b* Carrara, Nov 22, 1605; *d* Carrara, 1649), *Grove Art Online*, 2003, https://doi.org/10.1093/gao/9781884446054.article.T066088;
Peter Mellini, 'Pellegrini, Carlo [peud. Ape] (1839-1889)', H C G Matthew and Brian Harrison (eds), *Oxford Dictionary of National Biography*, Oxford University Press, 2004, https://doi.org/10.1093/ref:odnb/21806;
Leslie Ward, *Forty Years of 'Spy'*, London: Chatto & Windus, 1915

31
SIR HENRY DRUMMOND-WOLFF
Signed
Inscribed 'Drummond Wolf' and dated '5 Sept 74' on reverse
Watercolour
12 x 7 INCHES
Illustrated: *Vanity Fair*, 5 September 1874, Statesmen no 184,
'Consular Chaplains'

At the time of his appearance in *Vanity Fair*, Sir Henry
Drummond-Wolff (1830-1908) had just become MP for
Christchurch. He served in this role until 1880, when he became
MP for Portsmouth. In 1885, he was sent to Constantinople and
Egypt to negotiate as part of the Eastern Question and would
serve as the British High Commissioner in Egypt from 1885
to 1887.

COÏDÉ

James [Jacques-Joseph] Tissot (1836-1902), known also as 'Coïdé'

*'His work can hardly be called caricature; for the sketches were rather
characteristic and undoubtedly brilliant drawings of his subjects'*
(Sir Leslie Ward)

Though best known as the French painter of English society, James Tissot also produced insightful caricatures. These appeared in *Vanity Fair*, under the name 'Coïdé', in the period from 1869 to 1873, alongside those of 'Ape' and before the arrival of 'Spy'.

The second of four sons of a prosperous linen merchant, James Tissot was born in Nantes, on the River Loire, on 15 October 1836. He was educated at Jesuit colleges in Brugelette, Belgium; Vannes, Brittany; and Dôle, Franche-Comté. He considered becoming an architect and then an artist. Moving to Paris by 1856, he studied at the Ecole des Beaux-Arts, under Louis Lamothe and Hippolyte Flandrin. While there, he befriended James McNeill Whistler and Edgar Degas. Exhibiting at the Paris Salon from 1859 and at the Royal Academy, London, from 1864, he soon abandoned medieval subjects in favour of the elegant, polished, often complex, contemporary scenes for which he is best known. In 1869, he also began to produce his first caricatures for Thomas Gibson Bowles's society paper, *Vanity Fair*, signing them 'Coïdé', 'perhaps because they were a collaboration between Bowles's notions and Tissot's draughtsmanship, thus "co-idée"'(Richard Thomson, in Anna Gruetzner Robins and Richard Thomson, *Degas, Sickert and Toulouse-Lautrec. London and Paris 1870-1910*, London: Tate, 2005, page 20).

Following the outbreak of the Franco-Prussian War in 1870, Tissot fought in the defence of Paris, but fled to London a year later. Through the auspices of Bowles, he made many professional and social connections, and his work gained rapid popularity. He lived openly with his Irish mistress, Kathleen Newton, in a house in Grove End Road, St John's Wood. However, this sojourn came to an end in 1882 when, having contracted tuberculosis, she committed suicide at the age of 28.

Tissot returned to France, and soon turned to religion, both as a way of life and a subject for his art. He even made two visits to the Holy Land, in 1886-87 and 1889, which inspired a large series of watercolour illustrations of the Bible. These drawings were exhibited at the Doré Gallery on his return. On 8 August 1902, he died at the Château de Buillon, Doubs, Franche- Comté, which he had inherited from his father in 1888.

His work is represented in numerous public collections, including the National Portrait Gallery and Tate; Musée d'Orsay; and Brooklyn Museum (New York) and the Minneapolis Institute of Arts.

Further reading:

Willard E Misfeldt, 'Tissot, James [Jacques-Joseph] (*b* Nantes, 15 Oct 1836, *d* Château de Buillon, Doubs, 8 Aug 1902)', Jane Turner (ed), *The Dictionary of Art*, London: Macmillan, 1996, vol 31, pages 29-31

32
GENERAL TROCHU, 'THE HOPE OF FRANCE'
Ink and watercolour with pencil and chalk
11 ¾ x 7 INCHES
Illustrated: *Vanity Fair*, 17 September 1870

Louis-Jules Trochu (1815-1896) had served with distinction in the French armed forces during the Crimean War. During the Franco-Prussian War, he was appointed Governor of Paris and Commander-in-Chief of all forces responsible for the defence of the capital. The leadership he demonstrated during the Siege of Paris saw him named President of the Government of National Defence, the de facto head of state, on 4 September 1870.

SPY

Sir Leslie Ward, RP (1851-1922), known as 'Spy'

For almost 40 years, Sir Leslie Ward defined the look of the society paper, *Vanity Fair*. His well observed, meticulously conceived cartoons permanently altered the art of caricature in England. From the cruel and often grotesque caricatures made popular by the likes of Gillray and Daumier, Leslie Ward made caricature acceptable and, indeed, necessary to the who's who of Victorian high society.

Leslie Ward was born at Harewood Square, London (on the site of what is now Marylebone Station), on 21 November 1851. He was exposed to the artistic life from birth as his father, Edward Matthew Ward, and mother, Henrietta Ada Ward, were both professional artists. His father produced historical paintings and his mother was a fashionable painter of portraits. Indeed, the artistic tradition of Ward's family stretched back further still. His maternal grandfather, George Raphael Ward, was a mezzotint engraver and miniature painter, his mother's great-uncle was John Jackson RA, portrait painter in ordinary to William IV, and his great-grandfather, James Ward, was a versatile painter of landscapes, animals and portraits, engraver, lithographer and modeller. His godfather, Charles Robert Leslie, after whom he was named, was also a Royal Academician and father to George Dunlop Leslie, who won the Royal Academy Schools Silver Medal in 1814.

Ward was strongly influenced by the artistic environment in which he found himself as a young child. At the age of four, he holidayed in Calais with his parents, and produced what he considered to be his first caricatures, of a number of French soldiers loitering at the docks. As his parents were popular and highly sociable in artistic circles, the young Ward was introduced to a great number of the Victorian period's most influential literary and artistic figures. The novelist, Wilkie Collins, was a close friend of his parents, as was his brother, Charles Allston Collins, one of the original members of the Pre-Raphaelite Brotherhood. Other artists who visited his parents' studios when he was child included Daniel Maclise, Sir Edwin Landseer, John Everett Millais and William Holman Hunt. Ward was also introduced to the Queen and Prince Consort, who made regular visits to the studio. One such visit was during the progress of one of his father's commissioned pictures, *The Visit of Queen Victoria to the Tomb of Napoleon I*, which was referred to in *The Spectator*'s review of the Royal Academy Summer Exhibition in 1858 as 'a stagey, flashy, vulgar affair, with scarcely a redeeming point'.

Leslie Ward enjoyed a happy childhood. While he was still young, the family moved from Harewood Square to Upton Park, Slough, a rural environment that he adored. His artistic surroundings nurtured his desire to become an artist. Despite this, and the fact the he was a regular sitter for his parents, Ward never received a single lesson from either. His father was actually keen to dissuade him from becoming an artist and wished to see him educated in a more traditional manner. Initially, he attended Chase's School, Salt Hill, near Slough. However, he did not stay long as the school was soon broken up due to the ill health of the headmaster. As a result, he was sent to study at Eton at a younger age than was planned. At the request of his father, his aptitude and love for drawing was not encouraged whilst he was at Eton. Nevertheless, he

Photograph portrait of Sir Leslie Ward, 1915

continued to indulge his passion, regularly drawing the school's masters and his fellow pupils, and so becoming Eton's unofficial caricaturist. While he was still young, the family returned to London, moving to Kent Villa, Kensington, a large house with two studios one on top of the other for his parents. On school holidays, he spent much of his time watching his parents work there, as well as at the temporary studio erected on the terrace of the House of Lords, where he watched his father paint frescoes for the Houses of Parliament.

At the age of 16, Ward turned his attention to modelling and started a bust of his younger brother, Wriothesley Russell Ward. Working on it in his holidays, he finished it in time to submit it to the Royal Academy, where it was accepted and exhibited at the Summer Exhibition of 1867. However, he chose not to follow up on this success, deeming the process too much of a physical and mental strain on him. As a young man, he also indulged in a growing interest in the stage. During his school holidays, he would assist at various playhouses across London by painting scenery and playing in small roles. He first appeared in front of a large audience at the Bijou Theatre in Bayswater as part of an amateur company called 'The Shooting Stars', comprised largely of Cambridge undergraduates.

After leaving school at the age of 16, Leslie Ward travelled to Paris with a group of friends, for little more reason than to enjoy himself and soak up the city's artistic atmosphere. However, his father's desire to see him installed in a secure vocation resulted in Ward entering the office of Sydney Smirke RA, to study architecture. Smirke was a highly respected architect, whose most well-known works include the Carlton Club and the Reading Room at the British Museum. However, the mechanical process of the profession did not appeal to Ward, and his period with Smirke only served to strengthen his resolve to become an artist. After a year, Smirke had completed his work on the exhibition galleries at the Royal Academy's Burlington House and decided to retire. During this time, Ward had been made a member of the Architecture Association, and his father arranged for him to continue his architectural studies with Edward Barry RA. However, when he was informed that his period of study with Barry would last for another five years, Ward declined the offer and resolved finally to tell his father that he wished to pursue a career as an artist. He found an ally in the painter and Royal Academician, William Powell Frith, a close family friend who agreed to mediate between Leslie Ward and his father. The intervention of Frith at last saw his father relent and give his blessing to his chosen career.

His first commission was to end in unfortunate circumstances. Through his father, Ward obtained work undertaking a series of interior drawings for a family friend, a Mrs Butler Johnson Munro. However, after three months' work, Mrs Butler Johnson Munro suddenly died, leaving Ward with just a five pound note he had been paid after his first day. He did not have the heart to send a claim for full payment to her executors.

A six-week visit to Lord Lytton at Knebworth, in the company of his parents, gave Ward his first real encouragement that he could succeed as an artist. During his stay, he painted a watercolour of Knebworth's great hall and had Lord Lytton sit for a portrait. (He also caricatured his host from memory.) On his return home, his painting of the great hall was accepted by the Royal Academy and, determined to win his father's approval, he began his preparation to enter the Royal Academy Schools. This preliminary course of instruction included study at the Slade School of Fine Art, under Professor Edward Poynter. In 1871, he entered the Royal Academy Schools as probationer in Architecture, before becoming a full-time student.

Much of his time at the Royal Academy was spent exhibiting portraits in oil and watercolour and he could easily have made a career in that field. Portraits that he exhibited at the Royal Academy included drawings of his brother, Wriothesley, and his sister, Beatrice. Though he exhibited great talent in portrait painting, and would be elected to the Royal Society of Portrait Painters in 1891, he still held a great love for caricature and continued to draw the various personalities who crossed his path.

Leslie Ward's association with the society paper, *Vanity Fair*, began with a garden party hosted by Lord Leven. Here, he observed the eminent zoologist, Professor Richard Owen, who was nicknamed 'Old Bones'. So taken by what he described as his 'antediluvian incongruity', he resolved to caricature him. At this time, Thomas Gibson Bowles, the founder of *Vanity Fair*, had grown dissatisfied with the artists working for him the absence of his main caricaturist, Carlo Pellegrini, and was searching for new cartoonists. John Everett Millais, having known of Leslie Ward's skill and enjoyment in creating caricatures and his admiration for *Vanity Fair*, called to see a collection of his work. Particularly taken with the caricature of 'Old Bones', he urged Ward to submit it to *Vanity Fair*. He did so, and it was accepted and published in 1873. The cartoon was unsigned, as Bowles did not approve of Ward's original idea for a signature. When Bowles handed Ward a dictionary and suggested he search for a pseudonym, the page fell open on the 'S's and his eye was caught by 'Spy'.

Following the publication of his first cartoon, Leslie Ward became a permanent staff member at *Vanity Fair* and he was able to turn his attention 'whole-heartedly and with infinite pleasure' to caricature. When he and *Vanity Fair*'s other great cartoonist, Carlo Pellegrini, were first introduced at a social event, Pellegrini jokingly told onlookers that he had taught Ward everything he knew. He laughed it off, knowing it not to be the case, but when numerous journalists believed it to be true and put it into print, Ward grew to regret not correcting the comment. Nevertheless, this first meeting began a lasting friendship and great mutual admiration.

'Spy' was an apt pseudonym for Ward, as he often found himself 'stalking' his subjects everywhere from the law courts and Houses of Parliament to society gatherings and theatres of London, before drawing them from memory. In his early days at *Vanity Fair*, he was often given subjects that were refused by Pellegrini, and his caricatures were often the result of hours of continual attempts, watching his subjects as they walked or drove past. In Thomas Gibson Bowles, Ward found a valuable ally when studying his subjects. As Ward explains, 'he was so thoroughly a man of the world and withal so tactful and resourceful that I was glad when we worked in company. It was a great help for me, and I was able to employ my attention in observing while he took the responsibility of conversations and entertainment of the subject entirely off my hands'. In January 1873, Ward received a commission from William Luson Thomas, editor of *The Graphic*, and contributed a number of portrait drawings to the paper, including those of Sir John Cockburn, Benjamin Disraeli, William Gladstone and Lord Leighton. In 1876, he left *The Graphic* and worked exclusively for *Vanity Fair* alongside Pellegrini. When Pellegrini died in 1889, Ward produced virtually every cartoon.

In 1874, his parents had left London and moved to Windsor. As Ward was required to stay in London, he took rooms in Connaught Street, and a studio in William Street, Lowndes Square. As his fame grew and his time became more precious, he began to require many of his subjects to come to this studio and sit for him. This procedure frequently irritated him, as his sitters often made requests as to how they should be portrayed, or complained about the final result. Nevertheless, he continued to accept commissions to produce portraits, partly because he remained greatly fond of the process of portrait painting, but also because it was well paid. In an 1897 interview given by Oliver Armstrong Fry, then editor of *Vanity Fair*, to Frank Banfield of *Cassell's Magazine*, it was reported that Ward received between £300 and £400 for a portrait. Later in life, he would regret not allowing himself more time to work in this genre.

The nature of his work and his association with such a reputable society magazine as *Vanity Fair* meant that Leslie Ward figured prominently in the upper echelons of Victorian society. In 1874, he joined the Arts Club in Hanover Square, whose members at the time included *Punch* cartoonists John Tenniel and Charles Keene. He later became a member of the Orleans Club, the Lotus Club and the Pelican Club. In 1876, he became one of the original members of the Beefsteak Club, a bohemian club founded by Archibald Stuart Wortley. He was elected an honorary member of the Lyric Club, and also joined the newly opened Fielding Club and the Gallery Club, held on Sunday nights at the Grosvenor Galleries. In July 1880, he was invited on a cruise aboard the HMS Hercules by the Duke of Edinburgh, who had seen and admired his caricature of the Admiral Sir Reginald MacDonald, which had appeared in *Vanity Fair*. In 1890, he was given the honour of a sitting by the Prince of Wales at Marlborough House.

After many years as a bachelor, Leslie Ward married in 1899 to society hostess Judith Topham-Watney, the only daughter of Major Richard Topham, of the 4th Queen's Own Hussars. They had initially courted some years earlier, only for her parents to block their engagement on the grounds that Ward was financially unworthy. However, in 1899 they happened to meet again on a train journey, their relationship was rekindled and they were married a few months later at St Michael's Church in Chester Square. Settling down together in Elizabeth Street, Belgravia, they had one daughter, Sidney.

In 1911, Leslie Ward resigned from *Vanity Fair*, ending an association with the paper that had lasted almost 40 years. He was soon approached by the paper, *The World*, who offered him not only the same pay that he received at *Vanity Fair*, but also permission to retain the rights of his original drawings. As a result, he was able to send a collection of his works to the Turin Exhibition at the request of Sir Isidore Spielmann, for which he received a Grand Prix. He also occasionally produced portraits for *Mayfair*, which Ward described as 'the only Society journal that I can recall having succeeded in any way on the lines of *Vanity Fair*' [*Forty Years of 'Spy'*, page 337]. In 1914, he was commissioned by the staff of the *Pall Mall Gazette* and *The Observer* to produce a portrait of their editor, James Louis Garvin.

In 1915, Leslie Ward published his autobiography, *Forty Years of 'Spy'*. He was knighted in 1918. He died suddenly of heart failure at 4 Dorset Square, London, on 15 May 1922.

His work is represented in the collections of the National Portrait Gallery.

Further reading:

Peter Mellini, 'Ward, Sir Leslie [pseud. Spy] (1851-1922)', H C G Matthew and Brian Harrison (eds), *Oxford Dictionary of National Biography*, Oxford University Press, 2004, vol 57, pages 325-326;
Leslie Ward, *Forty Years of 'Spy'*, London: Chatto & Windus, 1915

33

HM GEORGE, KING OF GREECE
Signed
Watercolour and bodycolour with
pen and ink on tinted paper
12 × 7 ¼ INCHES
Illustrated: *Vanity Fair*, 21 October 1876, Sovereigns no 12

Spy's caricature of King George is a reminder of British, and generally international, involvement in the governance of Greece following its independence from the Ottoman Empire in 1830. At the London Conference in 1832, The 'Great Powers' – Britain, France and Russia – recognised the country's autonomy and established a monarchy in Greece under the Bavarian prince, Otto. He reigned for 30 years, but became increasingly unpopular with native Greek politicians, and was deposed in 1862. He was replaced at the suggestion of the Great Powers by the 17 year old Danish prince, William (1845-1913). He was elected the King of the Hellenes in 1863, and took the regnal name of George. At his urging, Greece adopted a more democratic constitution, and greatly developed its parliamentary process.

In the same year, his sister, Alexandria, married (Albert) Edward, the Prince of Wales and future Edward VII. These personal bonds further strengthened relations between Britain and Greece, and helped maintain George's reputation among the British people, as exemplified by Spy's gentle caricature, which was published in 1876.

During the nineteenth century there was a desire in Greek politics to unify all areas that had been historically inhabited by the ethnically Greek people. So, in 1897, the Greek population of Crete rose up against its Ottoman rulers, and the Greek Prime Minister, Theodoros Diligiannis, mobilised troops, which invaded Crete and crossed the Macedonian border into the Ottoman Empire. When Greece lost the war that followed, King George considered abdicating. However, when he survived an assassination attempt in 1898, his subjects began to hold him in greater esteem. In 1901, on the death of Queen Victoria he became the second-longest-reigning monarch in Europe.

In 1912, the Kingdom of Montenegro declared war against the Ottoman Empire, Crown Prince Constantine led the victorious Greek forces in support of the Ottoman Empire, in what became known as the First Balkan War. George planned to abdicate in favour of his son immediately after the celebration of his Golden Jubilee in October 1913. However, while walking in Thessaloniki on 18 March 1913, he was assassinated by the anarchist, Alexandros Schinas. Constantine succeeded to the throne.

34
REV HENRY MONTAGU VILLIERS
Signed
Watercolour and bodycolour with pencil
12 × 7 ½ INCHES
Illustrated: *Vanity Fair*, 21 August 1902, Men of the Day
no 847

Henry Montagu Villiers (1837-1908) held the office of
Prebendary of St Paul's Cathedral and later served as the Vicar
of St Paul's Church, Knightsbridge.

35
COL CHARLES NAPIER STURT
Signed
Watercolour with bodycolour on tinted paper
12 x 7 ¼ INCHES
Illustrated: *Vanity Fair*, 25 November 1876, Men of the Day
no 142, 'A Younger Son'

Charles Napier Sturt (1832-1886) was Conservative MP for
Dorchester in the period 1856-74. As a Lieutenant-Colonel in the
Grenadier Guards, he was severely wounded in 1854 at the
Battle of Inkerman, during the Crimean War.

36

COLONEL WILLIAM CORNWALLIS-WEST MP

Signed

Watercolour with bodycolour

15 ½ x 7 ½ INCHES

Illustrated: *Vanity Fair*, 16 July 1892, Statesmen no 595, 'Denbighshire'

Exhibited: 'The Long Nineteenth Century: Treasures and Pleasures',
Chris Beetles Gallery, London, March-April 2014, no 140

William Cornwallis-West (1835-1917) was born in Florence, the youngest child of Frederick West of Ruthin Castle, Denbighshire. Following his education – at Eton and Lincoln's Inn – he returned to Florence and developed his talent as a painter, gaining a reputation as a copyist, and also collecting. On the early death of his elder brother, Frederick, in 1868, he succeeded to the estate of Ruthin, and four years later married 17 year-old Mary Fitzpatrick, who would become a leading socialite (and later have an affair with the Prince of Wales). They shared their time between Ruthin and 49 Eaton Place.

West became High Sheriff of Denbighshire (1872), Lord-Lieutenant of Denbighshire (1872-1917), a Justice of the Peace and Honorary Colonel in the 4th battalion of the Royal Welch Fusiliers, and was awarded the Royal Naval Volunteer Reserve Officers' decoration. In 1885 he was returned to parliament for Denbighshire West, a seat he held until 1892, first as a Liberal and then as a Liberal Unionist.

On the death of his mother in 1886, West came into possession of Newlands Manor, Lymington, Hampshire, and attempted to develop the resort of Milford on Sea in emulation of the Duke of Devonshire's project at Eastbourne.

His children included George, who was the second husband of Jennie Jerome, mother of Winston Churchill, and then the second husband of the actress, Mrs Patrick Campbell; Daisy, Princess of Pless; and Constance Edwina, Duchess of Westminster.

37

THE EARL OF SHREWSBURY AND TALBOT

Signed

Watercolour and bodycolour

12 ¼ × 8 ¼ INCHES

Illustrated: *Vanity Fair*, 30 July 1903, Statesmen no 758, 'Cabs'

When only seventeen years old, Major Charles Chetwynd-Talbot (1860-1921) inherited the titles of the 20th Earl of Shrewsbury, 20th Earl of Waterford and 5th Earl of Talbot. Passionate about equestrian sports, he developed an interest in horse-drawn transport and, in London in 1888, founded the Shrewsbury and Talbot Cab and Noiseless Tyre Company; this would grow to 210 cabs and 365 horses. Following his separation from his wife in 1896, she remained at Alton Towers, Staffordshire, while he went to live at Ingestre Hall, in the same county. There, in 1903, he founded the Talbot car company in order to import the French Clément car into Britain, which began in 1905. Domestically designed Talbot cars followed from 1906.

38
LORD KENSINGTON, MP
Signed
Ink and watercolour with bodycolour and pencil
13 ¼ × 7 ¾ INCHES
Illustrated: *Vanity Fair*, 7 September 1878, Statesmen
no 281, 'A Whip'

William Edwardes (1835-1896) was Liberal MP for
Haverfordwest in Pembrokeshire during the period 1868-85.
Though succeeding to the title of Baron Kensington in the
Peerage of Ireland in 1872, he remained in the House of
Commons, as a Whip, a member of the Privy Council and,
latterly, Comptroller of the Household (1880-85). Created 1st
Baron Kensington in the Peerage of the United Kingdom in
1886, he then entered the House of Lords, and acted as its
Liberal Chief Whip in 1892-96.

39

SIR WALTER FRANCIS HELY-HUTCHINSON,
GOVERNOR OF NATAL, SOUTH AFRICA

Signed

Watercolour with bodycolour on tinted paper

6 ¾ × 12 ¼ INCHES

Illustrated: *Vanity Fair*, 7 July 1898, Men of the Day no 717, 'Natal'

Spy depicts Sir Walter Hely-Hutchinson wearing the Regalia of the
Most Distinguished Order of St Michael and St George.

40
JUDICIAL POLITENESS
THE RT HON SIR C S C BOWEN
Signed
Watercolour and bodycolour
12 × 10 INCHES
Illustrated: *Vanity Fair*, 12 March 1892

After being called to the bar at Lincoln's Inn in 1861, Charles Synge Christopher Bowen first rose to prominence as part of the prosecution team in the Tichborne Case, a cause célèbre that captured the public imagination in the late 1860s and early 1870s. In 1879 he was appointed a High Court judge in the Queen's Bench and in 1882 was raised to the position of Lord Justice of Appeal. In 1893, the year after his portrait appeared in *Vanity Fair*, he was made a Lord of Appeal in Ordinary and a life peer with the title Baron Bowen. In his youth, he played a single first-class cricket match for Hampshire against the MCC. He is credited with coining the phrase 'the man on the Clapham omnibus'.

41

MR FRANK LOCKWOOD, QC MP

Signed

Watercolour and pencil on tinted paper

7 ½ x 12 INCHES

Illustrated: *Vanity Fair*, 20 August 1887, Statesmen
no 526, 'York'

Frank Lockwood (1846-1897) was a famous lawyer and Liberal
MP for York in the period 1885-97. Having been called to the bar
in 1872, he went on to become Solicitor-General in Lord
Rosebery's ministry for the year 1894-95, and was knighted at
the same time. A talented amateur artist, he published the
Frank Lockwood Sketch-book in 1898.

42

SIR JAMES TAYLOR INGHAM, MA KT
Signed
Watercolour with bodycolour and pencil
16 ¼ × 10 ¾ INCHES
Provenance: The Dibben Family, Nash Priory and
4 Smith Square, London SW1
Illustrated: *Vanity Fair*, 20 February 1886, Men of the Day
no 353, 'Bow Street'

Yorkshire-born James Taylor Ingham (1805-1890) was
called to the bar at the Inner Temple, and initially joined
the northern circuit. Becoming a magistrate in London in
1849, he was made Chief Magistrate of London in 1876,
sitting at Bow Street. Later that year, he was knighted at
Osborne House.

43

LINLEY SAMBOURNE

Signed

Inscribed with title and dated 'Nov 1891'
below mount

Watercolour with bodycolour

12 ½ × 9 INCHES

Illustrated: *Vanity Fair*, 16 January 1892,
Men of the Day no 528, 'Sammy'

Linley Sambourne was an artist, cartoonist
and illustrator, who would succeed
Sir John Tenniel as the political cartoonist
of *Punch*. For a full biography of Linley
Sambourne, please refer to *The Illustrators*,
2015, page 34.

44
LORD RAGLAN
GEORGE FITZROY HENRY SOMERSET
Signed
Watercolour with bodycolour and pencil
14 x 7 ½ INCHES
Illustrated: *Vanity Fair*, 14 February 1901, Statesmen no 732

Shortly before his portrait appeared in *Vanity Fair*, the Lord Raglan
George Somerset had, in November 1900, been appointed Under-Secretary
for War in Lord Salisbury's Conservative government. His grandfather,
Lord FitzRoy Somerset, had served under the Duke of Wellington during
the Napoleonic Wars, losing an arm at Waterloo in 1815. He was made
Field Marshall of the British Armed Forces in the Crimea, where, in 1854,
he was partly responsible for the ill-fated 'Charge of the Light Brigade'.
George Somerset continued the military tradition of his family by joining
the Grenadier Guards and seeing action in the Second Anglo-Afghan War,
where he was decorated. In 1902, after serving as Under-Secretary for War,
he was appointed Lieutenant Governor of the Isle of Man.

45
CLEMENT KING SHORTER
THREE EDITORS
Signed
Inscribed 'Clement Shorter Esq' below mount
Watercolour with bodycolour on tinted paper
11 ½ × 7 INCHES
Illustrated: *Vanity Fair*, 24 December 1894,
Men of the Day no 607

A journalist and editor, Clement King Shorter began his
career as a sub-editor for the *Penny Illustrated Paper* and
columnist for the *Star* whilst working as a clerk in the
Exchequer and Audit Department at Somerset House.
In 1891, following the retirement of the editor of
The Illustrated London News, John Lash Latey, Shorter
offered himself to the director, William Ingram, for the
role and was accepted. Together with Ingram, he
founded and became editor of *The Sketch* in 1892 and,
following its acquisition by Ingram in 1893, editor of
The English Illustrated Magazine. In the years following his
appearance in *Vanity Fair*, he would become founder and
editor of *The Sphere* (1900) and *Tatler* (1901).

46

LORD STANLEY OF ALDERLEY
Signed
Inscribed with title and dated 'Oct 1st 1883' below mount
Watercolour with bodycolour
10 ½ x 7 ¼ INCHES
Drawn for but not illustrated in: *Vanity Fair*

Henry Stanley, 3rd Baron Stanley of Alderley (1827-1903), was a historian specialising in European exploration and expansion of the sixteenth century. He was Vice-President of the Hakluyt Society, which published his editions and translations, including Ferdinand Magellan's *The First Voyage Round the World* (1874).

Fascinated by all things oriental from a young age, Stanley showed an interest in Arabic while at Eton and – as a confident linguist – began to read it at Cambridge. Leaving university after a year, he became précis writer to Lord Palmerston, the foreign secretary, and worked in various positions in the diplomatic service for over a decade. In 1859, he left the service in order to travel in the Near East and Asia, and reached as far as Indonesia. It was also rumoured that he visited Mecca in order to convert to Islam. Continuing to travel through the 1860s, he made a secret Islamic marriage in 1862, to a Spanish woman, Fabia Fernandez Funes. (They underwent further marriage ceremonies at the register office at St George, Hanover Square, in 1869, and at St Alban's Roman Catholic Church, Macclesfield, in 1874. Only after her death in 1905 was it discovered that Fabia was a bigamist, who had already married in 1851, and whose husband did not die until 1870.)

In 1869, Stanley succeeded his father as the 3rd Baron Alderley and took his place in the House of Lords. However, while intending to announce his conversion to Islam, he seems not to have done so and, despite speaking on questions relating to religion and to India, failed to impress his fellow peers.

As a result of his Muslim principles, he closed the public houses on his Cheshire estate, and ensured that churches built or restored on his land, such as that at Llanbadrig, Anglesey, used exclusively geometrical glass. He was also buried according to Muslim rites.

His nephew, Bertrand Russell, described him as 'definitely stupid', but Muriel E Chamberlain, writing in the *Oxford Dictionary of National Biography*, has countered that he was 'brilliant, eccentric, and unstable' (Matthew and Harrison 2004, vol 52, page 214).

47

IAN CHARLES, 8TH EARL OF SEAFIELD

SHEEP

Signed, inscribed 'Vanity Fair' and dated 'Sept. 29. 1883'
Inscribed 'This picture belongs to Lady Nina Knowles,
presented by the artist 'Spy' – Dec 1917' on reverse
Watercolour and bodycolour
13 ¾ × 7 ¾ INCHES
Illustrated: Similar to *Vanity Fair*, 29 September 1883,
Statesmen no 434'

Ian Charles Ogilvy-Grant was a Conservative politician and
the 27th Chief of Clan Grant. His portrait in *Vanity Fair* is
titled 'Sheep' after the nickname given to him while he was
serving in the First Regiment of Life Guards between 1869
and 1877. He sat in the House of Lords until his death at the
age of 32, just a few months after he appeared in *Vanity Fair*.
As he was unmarried and childless, the earldom passed to his
uncle, James Ogilvy-Grant. The present portrait was produced
by Leslie Ward in 1917 as a gift to Lady Nina Knowles, the
daughter of Francis Ogilvy-Grant, the 10th Earl of Seafield.

48
EGERTON CASTLE
HE INSISTS THAT HIS PEN IS MIGHTIER THAN HIS SWORD
Signed
Watercolour and bodycolour
14 x 8 INCHES
Illustrated: *Vanity Fair*, 9 March 1905

Born into a wealthy publishing family, Egerton Castle was an author and swordsman, and was a leading figure in the revival of the art of historical fencing. In 1885, he wrote *Schools and Masters of Fencing: From the Middle Ages to the Eighteenth Century*, the standard reference on the sport, and captained the British epeé and sabre teams at the 1908 Olympic Games. He also found fame as writer of fiction, co-authoring several novels with his wife, Agnes. A number of these novels, including *The Pride of Jennico* (1897), *Rose of the World* (1905) and *The Bath Comedy* (1900), were later adapted into silent films.

Brock Brothers

BROCK BROTHERS

C E BROCK
Charles Edmund Brock, RI (1870-1938)

H M BROCK
Henry Matthew Brock, RI (1875-1960)

While retaining distinct artistic personalities, the brothers, Charles and Henry Brock, developed a mutually supportive working relationship. As a result, they became leading illustrators of historical subjects, and especially of eighteenth and early nineteenth-century literature.

For many generations, the Brock family farmed an area lying a dozen miles to the south of Cambridge. This tradition was broken by Edmund Brock who, as a reader in medieval and oriental languages for Cambridge University Press, lived in London and later in Cambridge itself. In turn, none of his seven children returned to farming. Of those that embarked on some kind of artistic career, the most successful were the illustrators, Charles and Henry.

Charles Brock was born in Holloway, London, on 5 February 1870. Soon after the birth of the second son, Richard, the family moved to Cambridge, and Henry was born there on 11 July 1875. Brought up in a strict Protestant tradition, the children went regularly to the Zion Chapel and attended the local Church of England School before moving to Cambridge Grammar School. Despite their great aptitude for art from an early age, neither Charles nor Henry attended art school. Charles studied for a while under the sculptor, Henry Wiles, but Henry developed through his close association with Charles who, even after leaving his family home, returned every day to work in its studio.

Charles illustrated books from 1891 and established himself three years later with an edition of *Gulliver's Travels* published by Macmillan. In the same year, Henry embarked on his career by working with Charles on the illustrations to a history textbook, also for Macmillan. This encouraged the publisher to commission both Charles and Henry as contributing illustrators to a new project, the 'Macmillan Standard Novels', alongside such established figures as Hugh Thomson. In 1895, Charles came into direct competition with Thomson when he was asked to illustrate Austen's *Pride and Prejudice* for this series. In the same decade, Charles and Henry also illustrated an edition of Austen's novels (Dent), so impressing their vision of eighteenth and nineteenth century England upon the public.

At the turn of the century, the Brock family moved to Arundine House, making it their permanent home and soon building a large studio in its garden. Here the brothers assembled the large collection of 'props' that enabled them

to develop a degree of historical accuracy much greater than that of their model Hugh Thomson, and so dominate the so-called 'costume' school.

Though they worked side by side, and often illustrated different editions of the same book, Charles and Henry still managed to project distinct artistic personalities. Charles produced a delicate, often broken, line that retained something of the quality of his original sketches; it is perhaps best exemplified by his drawings for *The Works of Thackeray* and *The Works of Lamb* (both 1902-3). Against this delicacy may be set Henry's strong sense of design, put to good use in a large number of cartoons for *Punch* (1905-60) and posters for the D'Oyly Carte Opera Company (1920s).

If Charles was the more technically versatile, sometimes working in oil, Henry tackled a wider range of subjects, being well known as an illustrator of stories of adventure (including those by Stevenson and Scott). And despite their affinity and mutual affection, Henry had to continue to work long after the death of his brother. Charles died in Cambridge on 28 February 1938, while Henry retired only in 1950, when his eyesight began to fail. He died on 21 July 1960. The brothers had both been elected to the membership of the Royal Institute of Painters in Water Colours, Henry in 1906, Charles two years later, in 1908.

H M BROCK
Henry Matthew Brock, RI
(1875-1960)

49 (opposite)
HOP O' MY THUMB
Signed
Ink and watercolour, 13 ½ × 10 INCHES

These illustrations (Nos *50-55*) were probably drawn for Seeley's *Elzevir* series. Seeley & Co, founded in 1744, was one of Britain's oldest and longest standing publishing firms. Amongst its many publications were reprintings of works published in the 17th and 18th centuries by the Dutch publishers, Elzevir.

50
JOHN MILTON
Signed
Inscribed with title below mount
Pencil and watercolour
6 ½ x 5 ¼ INCHES

51
MONTAIGNE
Signed
Inscribed with title below mount
Watercolour with ink
6 ½ x 5 ½ INCHES

52
GOLDSMITH
Signed
Inscribed with title below mount
Watercolour with crayon
6 ¼ × 5 INCHES

53
WILLIAM BLAKE
Signed
Inscribed with title below mount
Watercolour with pencil, crayon and ink
7 × 5 ½ INCHES

54
REVEREND R H BARHAM
Signed
Inscribed with title below mount
Watercolour and crayon
6 ½ × 4 ½ INCHES

55
DE QUINCEY:
CONFESSIONS OF AN ENGLISH OPIUM EATER
Signed
Inscribed with title below mount
Watercolour with crayon and bodycolour
6 ¾ × 4 ¾ INCHES

C E BROCK
Charles Edmund Brock, RI (1870-1938)

THE LAST ESSAYS
OF ELIA

The *Last Essays of Elia* was the second volume of essays written by Charles Lamb, published in 1833 by Edward Moxon following the publication of *Essays of Elia* in 1823. These editions were complied from Charles Lamb's essays that had first begun appearing in *The London Magazine* between 1820 and 1825, which he had written under the pseudonym 'Elia'.

56
THE SUPERANNUATED MAN
Signed, inscribed with title and dated 1899
Inscribed 'Last Essays of Elia' below mount
Ink
9 ¼ x 7 INCHES
Illustrated: Charles Lamb, *Last Essays of Elia*, London: J M Dent & Sons, 1900, page 86

57

THE PITIABLE INFIRMITIES OF OLD MEN
Signed and dated 1899
Inscribed with title and 'Stage Illusion. Last Essays of Elia. p 193'
below mount
Ink
9 ¼ × 7 ¾ INCHES
Illustrated: Charles Lamb, *Last Essays of Elia*, London: J M Dent
& Sons, 1900, page 28

58

STAGE ILLUSION
Signed with initials, inscribed with title and dated 1899
Inscribed 'Last Essays of Elia. Headpiece' below mount
Ink
7 × 8 ½ INCHES
Illustrated: Charles Lamb, *Last Essays of Elia*, London: J M Dent & Sons, 1900, page 25

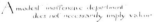

59
A MODEST INOFFENSIVE DEPORTMENT DOES
NOT NECESSARILY IMPLY VALOUR
Signed, inscribed with title and dated 1899
Inscribed 'Popular Fallacies. No 1' below mount
Ink
11 ¾ × 7 INCHES
Illustrated: Charles Lamb, *Last Essays of Elia*, London:
J M Dent & Sons, 1900, page 211

60
LIGHTED OUT THE RELIC FROM HIS DUSTY TREASURES
Signed and dated 1899
Inscribed with title and 'Last Essays of Elia. Old China' below mount
Ink
5 ¾ × 5 ¼ INCHES
Illustrated: Charles Lamb, *Last Essays of Elia*, London: J M Dent & Sons,
1900, page 190

61

YOUR TALL
DISPUTANTS
HAVE ALWAYS
THE ADVANTAGE
Signed with initials and
dated 1899
Inscribed with title and
'Popular Fallacies VII.
Of two disputants,
the warmest is
generally in the wrong'
below mount
Ink
7 × 7 ½ INCHES
Illustrated: Charles
Lamb, *Last Essays of
Elia*, London: J M
Dent & Sons, 1900,
page 220

62

NEW YEAR'S BAT
Inscribed 'Tailpiece to New Year's Coming
of Age'
Ink
2 × 4 ½ INCHES
Illustrated: Charles Lamb, *Last Essays of Elia*,
London: J M Dent & Sons, 1900, page 172

63

IT HAS LEARNED TO GO TO MARKET
Signed and dated 1899
Inscribed with title and 'Last Essays of Elia. Popular Fallacies XII'
below mount
Ink; 8 ¾ × 6 INCHES
Illustrated: Charles Lamb, *Last Essays of Elia*, London: J M Dent & Sons, 1900,
page 235

Fairy & Fantasy

FAIRY & FANTASY

FLORENCE HARRISON

Florence Susan Harrison (1877-1955)

Florence Harrison's fantasical illustrations for children combined Pre-Raphaelite influences with the practices of fin-de-siècle poster artists. Associated with the publisher, Blackie and Son, throughout her career, Florence Harrison's work ranged from illustrations of her own poetry for children, to Romantic literary texts by Rossetti, Tennyson and Morris, to one of her most celebrated creations, the 1912 book, *Elfin Song.*

For a biography of Florence Harrison, please refer to *The Illustrators*, 2014, page 146

Further reading:

Mary Jacobs, 'Florence Susan Harrison', *Studies in Illustration*, Imaginative Book Illustration Society, no 46, winter 2010, pages 22-59 (with a bibliography of published illustrations)

Nos **64-75** are all executed in ink and are all illustrated in Florence Harrison, *Elfin Song*, London: Blackie & Son, 1912

64
THE FAIRY FLOWERS IN HER HAND
4 ¼ x 2 ½ inches
Illustrated: page 82, 'The Changelings'

65 *(above)*
AND SO HE CALLED A LITTLE BOY
2 x 2 ¼ inches
Illustrated: page 41, 'The Gargoyle and the Chestnut Tree'

67 *(below right)*
ONE I KNOW, ONE I KNOW, WHO HAS NEVER SEEN THE SNOW
4 ¼ x 3 ½ inches
Illustrated: page 59, 'A Snowy Day'

66
THE FAIRY FLOWERS IN HER HAND
4 ¼ x 2 ½ inches
Illustrated: page 82, 'The Changelings'

68 *(above left)*
FAIRIES PLAYING BY THE MOON
3 ¼ x 2 ½ INCHES
Illustrated: page 6

69 *(above centre)*
PLAYING A PIPE
4 ½ x 2 ½ INCHES
Illustrated: last page

70 *(above)*
OR AS A RIVER REED
SOME WATER-FAIRY
GATHERS TO MAKE A FLUTE
FOR MUSIC AIRY
5 x 3 INCHES
Illustrated: page 127, 'The Runaway
Snowman'

71 *(left)*
HE TURNED HIS GENTLE HEAD
AND SAW US STEALING IN
4 ½ x 7 ½ INCHES
Illustrated: page 119, 'A Christmas Dream'

72
FAIRY IN A
ROSE BUSH
3 ¼ x 7 INCHES
Illustrated: page 12

73 (left)
THEIR EARS SO POINTED,
LONG, AND THIN
2 ¼ x 2 ¾ INCHES
Illustrated: page 85, 'The Changelings'

74 (right)
WILL YOU COME AND LIVE WITH
ME IN MY LITTLE NURSERY
Inscribed with title below mount
5 x 3 INCHES
Illustrated: page 73, 'Thistle Tassel'

75
WE WILL WORK FOR
YOU WITH PLEASURE
2 x 5 ½ INCHES
Illustrated: page 90, 'Pixy Work'

HONOR APPLETON

Honor Appleton (1879-1951)

Honor Appleton represented childhood innocence without resorting to sentimentality, most notably in her illustrations to Mrs Cradock's 'Josephine' stories. These are, for the most part, an exquisitely naturalistic depiction of a young girl's life, with occasional, but increasing suggestions that her dolls are also alive.

Honor Appleton was born at 30 St Michael's Place, Brighton, Sussex, on 4 February 1879, the third of four children of the Revd John Appleton and his wife, Georgina (née Wilkie). By 1891, her father had died, and she had moved with her mother and siblings to London, and had settled at 41 Edith Road, Fulham, London. Having shown a talent for art from an early age, she studied at the National Art Training School, South Kensington, and then at Frank Calderon's School of Animal Painting, at 54 Baker Street, where she gained a scholarship. This was followed by a brief period in the studio of Sir Arthur Cope RA.

In January 1901, Appleton enrolled at the Royal Academy Schools, at the same time as her elder sister, Alice. She seems to have attended intermittently until 1906, during which time her work was recommended by John Watson Nichol. She also involved herself in the social life of the schools, by joining its Ladies Hockey Club. She was skilled at the game, and also played for Sussex, her home county. While still a student, Appleton began her career as an illustrator, publishing *The Bad Mrs Ginger* with Grant Richards in 1902. Evolving her own distinctive style through the assimilation of such nursery artists as Kate Greenaway, Annie French and early Mabel Lucie Attwell, she established herself professionally eight years later with Blake's *Songs of Innocence* (Herbert and Daniel, 1910).

By 1911, Appleton was living at 3 Ventnor Villas, Hove, Sussex, with her mother and elder sister, Rachel, and she remained at that address throughout her career. Shrewd and independent, she travelled only on matters of business, and was content to stay locally with her sister, Alice, and her husband in their home in Wivelsfield. She was active in her local community, both artistically and socially, and was a member of the Sussex Women's Art Club. During wartime, she worked as a nurse for the Civil Defence.

Continuing to keep herself well-informed about the work of her contemporaries, Appleton subscribed to Percy Bradshaw's correspondence course, *The Art of the Illustrator*, in 1917. During the following three decades she illustrated over 150 books. While the best known of her early illustrations were for the 'Josephine' series, published by Blackie, to texts by Mrs Cradock, she produced much other fine work. In the 1930s and 40s, she moved away from nursery subjects to concentrate upon children's versions of literary classics for George G Harrap.

She died at Brooklands Nursing Home, Haywards Heath, on 30 December 1951, and was the subject of a memorial show held at Hove Public Library in the following year.

Further reading:

Alan Horne, 'Appleton, Honor Charlotte (1879-1951)', H C G Matthew and Brian Harrison (eds), *Oxford Dictionary of National Biography*, Oxford University Press, 2004, https://doi.org/10.1093/ref:odnb/69285

The very successful exhibition of work by Honor Appleton which was held by Chris Beetles Gallery in 1990 was the very first since her memorial show in 1951. It was accompanied by a 72-page fully-illustrated catalogue, which included an essay and bibliography.

HONOR C APPLETON (1879-1951)

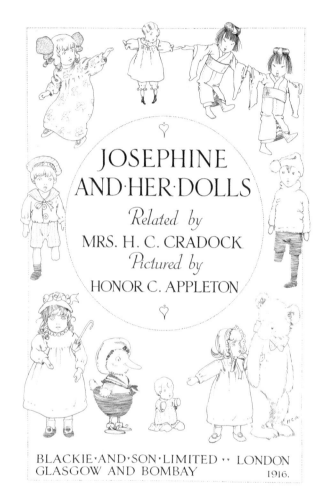

76
A BIT OF STRING DIVIDED THE ARMIES
Signed
Inscribed with title below mount
Watercolour with pencil
8 ½ × 6 ¼ INCHES
Illustrated: H C Craddock, *Josephine and Her Dolls*, London: Blackie and Son,
1916, frontispiece
Exhibited: 'Honor C Appleton (1879-1951)', Chris Beetles Gallery, London,
May 1990, no 5

77
JOSEPHINE'S DOLLS
Signed with initials
Ink
10 ½ × 7 INCHES
Illustrated: H C Craddock, *Josephine and Her Dolls*, London: Blackie
and Son, 1916, title page

78
HOW THEY HURRIED!
Signed
Inscribed with title below mount
Watercolour with bodycolour, 9 ½ × 7 INCHES
Illustrated: Mrs H C Cradock, *Josephine's Pantomime*, London: Blackie and
Son, 1939, facing page 14
Exhibited: 'Honor C Appleton (1879-1951)', Chris Beetles Gallery, London,
May 1990, No 217

79
WILLIAM PUT THE CAP ON HIS OWN HEAD
Signed and inscribed with title below mount
Watercolour with bodycolour
9 ½ × 7 ¼ INCHES
Exhibited: 'Honor C Appleton (1879-1951)', Chris Beetles Gallery,
May 1990, No 73;
'The Illustrators', The Brook Gallery, Budleigh Salterton Literary Festival,
September 2010

80

TOWARDS EVENING TIME .... OLE LUK-OIE COMES

Signed, inscribed with title and dated 1920

Watercolour

9 ¼ x 7 ¾ INCHES

81

AUTUMN

Signed and inscribed with title

Watercolour

5 ½ x 3 ¾ INCHES

EDMUND DULAC

Edmund Dulac (1882-1953)

The multi-talented artist, Edmund Dulac, contributed more than a dash of French panache to the illustration of English gift books. Developing an exquisite palette and eclectic style, that referenced Japanese prints and Persian miniatures, he complemented the work of his chief rival, Arthur Rackham.

For a biography of Edmund Dulac, please refer to *The Illustrators*, 2017, pages 63-64

His work is represented in numerous public collections, including the British Museum, the Cartoon Art Trust, the Imperial War Museum, the Museum of London, the Victoria and Albert Museum, the Fitzwilliam Museum (Cambridge); and the New York Public Library and Texas University.

Further reading:
Edmund Dulac: *Illustrator and Designer*,
Sheffield City Art Galleries, 1983;
James Hamilton, 'Dulac, Edmund [Edmond]
(1882-1953)', H C G Matthew and Brian Harrison
(eds), *Oxford Dictionary of National Biography*, Oxford
University Press, 2004, vol 17, pages 168-170;
Ann Conolly Hughey, *Edmund Dulac. His Book
Illustrations. A Bibliography*, Potomac: Buttonwood
Press, 1995; Colin White, *Edmund Dulac*, London:
Studio Vista, 1976

82

ISIDORE DE LARA
Signed, inscribed 'Apollon Isidoros'
in Greek and dated 1917
Signed, dedicated 'To S A Serenissime
Madame La Princesse de Monaco'
and dated 1917 below mount
Watercolour with bodycolour
13 ½ × 9 ¾ INCHES

In 1892 the song writer Isidore de Lara was praised for his opera, *The Light of Asia*. Seven years later he dedicated another opera, *Messaline*, to the Princess of Monaco.

MARGARET TARRANT

Margaret Winifred Tarrant (1888-1959)

From the late 1900s, Margaret Tarrant was preoccupied with chronicling innocent childhood in its many moods and its great variety of activities. From 1920, her talents were channelled by her most important business relationship, with the Medici Society, which still publishes her books, cards and calendars today. Though her approach could seem highly idealised, even romanticised, its success lies in the degree to which it was grounded in close observation and the discipline of drawing from life.

For a biography of Margaret Tarrant, please refer to *The Illustrators*, 2014, page 162

Further reading:

John Gurney, *Margaret Tarrant and Her Pictures*, London: The Medici Society, 1982;

Claire Houghton, 'Tarrant, Margaret Winifred (1888-1959)',

in H C G Matthew and Brian Harrison (eds), *Oxford Dictionary of National Biography*, Oxford University Press, 2004, vol 53, pages 791-792

83

ILLUSTRATED LETTER
Signed and dated '13 VIII 49'
Pencil and ink with watercolour on paper
8 × 5 ¼ INCHES

"Troon"
Wonham Way
Gomshall
13 VIII 49

Dear Mrs Schoemann

I was walking down the road today, and looking at some laurel leaves, I wondered whether they could be preserved in glycerine for the winter, as was suggested in the book you sent me. Suddenly I had a dreadful thought – I could not remember writing to thank you for it. Did I? If not, I am terribly sorry.

Margaret W Tarrant

84
TOM THUMB
Signed
Watercolour with ink and bodycolour
7 ¼ × 5 ½ INCHES
Exhibited: 'The Turn of Women Artists
1837-2018', Chris Beetles Gallery,
London, March-April 2018, no 142

DOROTHY FITCHEW
Dorothy Fitchew (1889-circa 1976)

Dorothy Fitchew was a landscape and figure painter and illustrator, specialising in natural history subjects.

Dorothy Fitchew was born in Camberwell, the daughter of the illustrator and art editor, Edward Hubert Fitchew (1851-1934). By 1910, the family was living at The Oriels, Widmore, Bromley, Kent. From there, she sent 'large and elaborate watercolours of Shakespearean and legendary subjects' (Simon Houfe) to the Royal Academy and other leading exhibition venues in the years 1911-15.

By 1930, Fitchew was working as an illustrator, in that year collaborating with Charles Folkard on an edition of nursery rhymes. Increasingly, she specialised in natural history subjects, her work as an illustrator appearing in such books as W J Stokoe's *Mother Nature's Wild Animals* (1939), S B Whitehead's *In Your Flower Garden* (1947) and M C Carey's *Wild Flowers at a Glance* (1949). She also wrote and illustrated *Good Health to the Garden* (1946).

By 1949, Fitchew was a member of the Quekett Microscopical Club, and living at 30 The Fairway, Bickley, Bromley, Kent. In 1976, the club's journal recorded her death.

Her work is represented in the collections of the Natural History Museum.

85
FAIRIES
DANCING
WITH A
GARLAND OF
FLOWERS
Signed
Ink and watercolour
13 ¼ × 18 INCHES

Early 20th Century
Illustrators & Cartoonists

EARLY 20TH CENTURY ILLUSTRATORS & CARTOONISTS

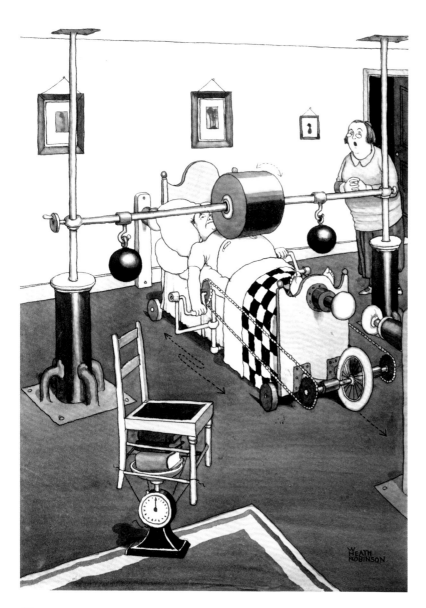

WILLIAM HEATH ROBINSON
William Heath Robinson (1872-1944)

Heath Robinson is a household name, and a byword for a design or construction that is 'ingeniously or ridiculously over-complicated' (as defined by *The New Oxford Dictionary of English*, 1998, page 848). Yet, he was also a highly distinctive and versatile illustrator, whose work could touch at one extreme the romantic watercolours of a Dulac or Rackham, at another the sinister grotesqueries of a Peake, and at yet another the eccentricities of an Emett.

For a biography of William Heath Robinson, please refer to *The Illustrators*, 2018, page 22.

Essays on various aspects of Heath Robinson's achievements have appeared in previous editions of *The Illustrators*: on his illustrations to *Rabelais* in 1996, pages 112-113; on the relationship of his illustrations to those of Arthur Rackham in 1997, pages 124-125; on his illustrations to *The Arabian Nights Entertainments* in 1999, pages 73-74; and on one of his illustrations to *Twelfth Night* in 2000, pages 17-18.

Geoffrey Beare, *William Heath Robinson*, London: Chris Beetles, 2011, fully illustrated catalogue, paperback, 163 pages

86

THE NEW BANTING BED FOR REDUCING THE FIGURE
Signed
Ink and watercolour
13 ¾ x 9 ¾ INCHES
Illustrated: *The Sunday Graphic*, 27 January 1929;
W Heath Robinson, *Absurdities. A Book of Collected Drawings*, London: Hutchinson & Co, 1934

The Chris Beetles Gallery has mounted a number of significant exhibitions of the work of William Heath Robinson, including:

1. 'William Heath Robinson (1872-1944)', Chris Beetles Gallery, March 1987 (with a fully illustrated catalogue)

2. 'The Brothers Robinson', Chris Beetles Gallery and the Royal Festival Hall, February 1992 (with a fully illustrated catalogue)

3. 'William Heath Robinson (1872-1944). 50th Anniversary Exhibition', Chris Beetles Gallery, September 1994

4. 'The Gadget King', Manchester City Art Galleries, Heaton Hall, May-October 2000

5. 'W Heath Robinson', Dulwich Picture Gallery, Linbury Room, November 2003 (to complement Dulwich's own exhibition of William Heath Robinson)

6. 'Heath Robinson at Nunnington Hall', National Trust, Nunnington Hall, North Yorkshire, July 2005

7. 'Contraptions. William Heath Robinson (1872-1944)', Chris Beetles Gallery, June-August 2007 (to launch a volume of cartoons published by Duckworth)

8. 'William Heath Robinson 1872-1944', Chris Beetles Gallery, May-June 2011 (with a fully illustrated catalogue – see catalogue image)

9. 'The Inventive Art of William Heath Robinson', Chris Beetles Gallery, March-April 2016

87
SIGNS OF CHRISTMAS
Signed and inscribed with title
Ink and watercolour
14 ½ x 9 ½ inches

MAX BEERBOHM
Sir Max Beerbohm (1872-1956)

Equally valued as a caricaturist and writer, Max Beerbohm sustained an elegant detachment in art and life. Though the tone of his drawings is often lightly wicked, it is also affectionate, for he hated to wound his subjects, most of whom he knew and liked. As a result, he was on safest ground in satirising artists and writers of the past, and in making many self-caricatures.

For a biography of Max Beerbohm, please refer to *The Illustrators*, 2014, page 89.

88
G K CHESTERTON
Inscribed 'G K C'
Pencil
9 ¼ x 6 ½ INCHES
Drawn on reverse of 'Villino Chiaro Rapallo' headed paper

89 *(opposite)*
PUBLICITY
MR SHAW TO THE LAUREATE: 'BRAVO! WITHOUT ANY BLARNEY, BRAVO! BUT LOOK HERE: YOU'LL NEVER CUT ME OUT UNLESS YOU BROADCAST.'
Signed, inscribed with title and dated 1929
Watercolour and ink
12 ¼ x 14 INCHES
Illustrated: *Manchester Guardian*, 23 November 1929
Exhibited: 'Sir Max Beerbohm', Leicester Galleries, London, 1952, no 138
Literature: Rupert Hart-Davis (compiler), *A Catalogue of the Caricatures of Max Beerbohm*, London: Macmillan, 1972, no 1511, page 136

The present work was executed after the publication of Robert Bridges' (poet laureate 1913-1930) 'The Testament of Beauty' in 1929. Robert Bridges and George Bernard Shaw were both members of the BBC Advisory Committee on Spoken English, but Shaw was also a successful broadcaster.

Publicity

Mr. Shaw, to the Laureate: "Bravo! Without any blarney, Bravo! But look here: you'll never cut me out unless you broadcast."

Max 1929

LAWSON WOOD
Lawson Wood RI (1878-1957)

Lawson Wood was an accomplished cartoonist, illustrator and poster designer. He gained great popularity with his humorous illustrations of animals, including dinosaurs and monkeys. The ginger ape, Gran'pop, proved a particular favourite on both sides of the Atlantic.

For a biography of Lawson Wood, please refer to *The Illustrators*, 2020, pages 46-47.

90
ALL SCOTCH
NO 6 ALL SCOTCH THRIFT. A BAG-PIPE CHAMPION REDUCING HIS GAS BILL
Signed and dated 23
Inscribed with title on reverse
Watercolour and bodycolour
14 × 10 INCHES

91
LEAVE THE REST TO US
Signed
Inscribed with title and 'Gran'pop up to date' on reverse
Watercolour
17 ¼ × 13 ¼ INCHES

92
ALL OUT FOR XMAS
Signed
Inscribed with title on reverse
Watercolour
14 ½ x 11 ¾ INCHES

93
SETTLING THE ANNUAL
ACCOUNTS
Signed
Inscribed with title on reverse
Watercolour
15 x 11 ¾ INCHES

MABEL LUCIE ATTWELL
Mabel Lucie Attwell
(1879-1964)

Mabel Lucie Attwell developed her own imaginative, and often amusing, imagery through annuals and postcards. Then, as her popularity increased, she applied it to a wide range of products. She was a household name by the 1920s, by which time no home was complete without an Attwell plaque or money-box biscuit tin.

For a biography of Mabel Lucie Attwell, please refer to *The Illustrators*, 2020, page 88

94
THE PIXIE PICNIC
Signed
Watercolour
13 ¼ x 10 ¾ INCHES

MABEL LUCIE ATTWELL'S BATHROOM PLAQUE

Every bathroom should have one, and for over fifty years most did.

Please remember – don't forget –
Never leave the bathroom <u>wet</u>. –

The washable bathroom plaque became the most popular image of this century's best loved illustrator, Mabel Lucie Attwell.

Nor leave the soap still in the water
That's a thing we <u>never</u> ought'er.

It sold in hundreds of thousands throughout half a century because it had all the elements that made Mabel Lucie Attwell a success: simplicity of design, striking colour, charm and cute kids, but above all a message. Mabel Lucie was an illustrator who knew how to communicate. The message was classless: between the Wars all levels of society bought it and hung it in the bathroom as a jokey talisman for good behaviour. It may be a piece of bossy doggerel but it is fun and was beloved of landladies from Blackpool to Bognor, hoping to soften the edge of their regimented homeliness.

Nor leave the towels about the floor,
Nor keep the bath an hour or more

From Cambridge to Kensington Gore mothers purchased it in order to control the bathing excesses of all the family, a Moses tablet for middle-class ablutions. Indeed, the nanny may have recited it to her pink-skinned charge and so insulated an even closer relationship between cleanliness and godliness, but it was essentially a message from the grown-ups to their soapy, soaking peers, an attempt to take the steam out of the family battleground.

When other folks are wanting one –
Please don't forget – it isn't done!

Mabel Lucie's dictums are from the mouths of babes and toddlers, but directed to the sophisticated and regulated adult world. The chubby, pink-cheeked and moon-faced little beings intoned the rhymes in all the pictures, but it was the carefully observed demeanour and posture of these cute archetypes that were the only childish components. The sentiments were for a world far less spontaneous.

Chris Beetles

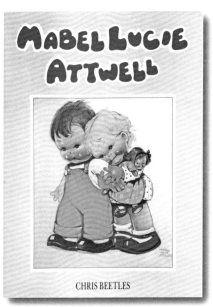

Chris Beetles, *Mabel Lucie Attwell*,
London: Chris Beetles Ltd, 1997

95

**I'M HOPING GOOD FAIRIES
ARE WELL ON THE WAY
TO BRING YOU GOOD
FORTUNE FOR EVERY DAY**
Watercolour and bodycolour
7 x 12 ¾ INCHES
Provenance: Estate of Mabel Lucie
Attwell and by descent
Illustrated: Design for Postcard no
2028, for Valentine of Dundee
Literature: Chris Beetles, *Mabel
Lucie Attwell*, London: Pavilion
Books, 1988, page 74-75;
John Henty, *The Collectable World of
Mabel Lucie Attwell*, London:
Richard Dennis, 1999, page 55
Exhibited: 'Mabel Lucie Attwell',
Chris Beetles Gallery, 1984, no 20

96

**PLEASANT DREAMS –
SWEET REPOSE
ALL THE BED – AND ALL
THE CLO'S**
Signed
Watercolour and bodycolour
7 ¾ x 12 ¾ INCHES
Provenance: Estate of Mabel Lucie
Attwell and by descent
Illustrated: Design for Postcard no
657, for Valentine of Dundee
Literature: Chris Beetles, *Mabel
Lucie Attwell*, London: Pavilion
Books, 1988, page 78-79;
John Henty, *The Collectable World of
Mabel Lucie Attwell*, London:
Richard Dennis, 1999, page 45

97
SLEEPY HEAD
Ink with pencil and bodycolour on board
8 ½ × 6 ¼ INCHES
Provenance: Estate of Mabel Lucie Attwell and by descent
Illustrated: Design for Postcard no 2828, for Valentine of Dundee, 1929
Literature: John Henty, *The Collectable World of Mabel Lucie Attwell*, London: Richard Dennis, 1999, page 61

98
AN' YOU KNOW WHAT MEN ARE!
Signed
Watercolour, bodycolour and pencil
11 ¼ × 9 ¼ INCHES
Provenance: Estate of Mabel Lucie Attwell and by descent
Illustrated: Design for Postcard no 335, for Valentine of Dundee
Literature: Chris Beetles, *Mabel Lucie Attwell*, London: Pavilion Books, 1988, page 29;
John Henty, *The Collectable World of Mabel Lucie Attwell*, London: Richard Dennis, 1999, page 43
Exhibited: 'Mabel Lucie Attwell', Chris Beetles Gallery, 1984, no 5

99
I'D LIKE TO SEE MORE
OF YOU – YOU SWEET
THING
Signed
Watercolour and bodycolour
7 ¼ x 10 ¼ INCHES
Provenance: Estate of Mabel
Lucie Attwell and by descent
Illustrated: Design for
Postcard no 615, for
Valentine of Dundee
Literature: John Henty, *The
Collectable World of Mabel
Lucie Attwell*, London:
Richard Dennis, 1999,
page 70

100
AUSTIN'S SEVEN
Signed
Watercolour and bodycolour
9 ¼ x 15 ¾ INCHES
Provenance: Estate of Mabel
Lucie Attwell and by descent
Illustrated: Design for
Postcard no 1299, for
Valentine of Dundee
Literature: Chris Beetles,
Mabel Lucie Attwell, London:
Pavilion Books, 1988, page
108-109;
John Henty, *The Collectable
World of Mabel Lucie Attwell*,
London: Richard Dennis,
1999, page 51
Exhibited: 'Mabel Lucie
Attwell', Chris Beetles
Gallery, 1984, no 70

101
DID YOU KNOW I'M ALSO A GOOD COOK?
Signed
Watercolour with bodycolour
9 ½ × 7 ¼ INCHES
Provenance: Estate of Mabel Lucie Attwell and by descent
Illustrated: Design for Postcard no 3277, for Valentine of Dundee
Literature: John Henty, *The Collectable World of Mabel Lucie Attwell*, London: Richard Dennis, 1999, page 63

102
KEEP ON KEEPING ON –
WOTEVER YOU DO IT IS SURE TO BE WRONG
Watercolour with bodycolour
13 × 9 ¼ INCHES
Provenance: Estate of Mabel Lucie Attwell and by descent
Illustrated: Design for Postcard no 3862, for Valentine of Dundee
Literature: John Henty, *The Collectable World of Mabel Lucie Attwell*, London: Richard Dennis, 1999, page 65

E H SHEPARD
Ernest Howard Shepard (1879-1976)

While E H Shepard is now best remembered for his immortal illustrations to *Winnie-the-Pooh* and *The Wind in the Willows*, he was a wide-ranging artist and illustrator, with an unsurpassed genius for representing children, and an underrated talent for political cartoons.

For a biography of E H Shepard, please refer to *The Illustrators*, 2018, page 41

For essays on various aspects of the artist's achievements, see *The Illustrators*, 1999, pages 151-152; *The Illustrators*, 2000, pages 28-32; and *The Illustrators*, 2007, pages 199-200

103
QUARRELLING THROUGH THE AGES
Signed twice
Ink
12 ½ x 19 INCHES

104 (opposite)
THEY BUILT SHIPS, 1953
Signed twice and inscribed
'To Keith Mackenzie from Ernest H Shepard Sept 1968' and 'The poem by C Fox Smith in *Punch* January 21st 1953'
Ink
13 x 10 INCHES
Illustrated: *Punch*, 21 January 1953

THEY BUILT SHIPS

NIGH the mouldering staithe
    Where the lads come to bathe,
And the tidal river as it passes
Licks with salty lips
The wiry grasses
Where the cattle graze,
There, in the old days,
They built ships...

Staunch little ships they built here,
Craft with coastwise rigs,
Schooners, ketches, brigs,
That sailed many a year
With their homely freights—
Cornish clay, granite, Bethesda slates—
To and fro between Fowey and Falmouth,
        Runcorn and Wales,
Dipping both rails under
        in the channel gales,
Beating up to wind'ard with the
        sunlight on their sails...

There were bustle and noise then,
Voices of boys and men,
And the clean shipyard smells
Of sawdust, paint and tar;
You could hear from far
Late and soon
The anvil's clang
And the caulker's mallets as they rang
All in time and tune,
Like a peal of bells...

But now its ended and done;
Thirty years agone
The last ship left the ways,
With her new hunting flying,
And the gulls crying
All round her, and the folk
    cheering from the river side
To see her take her tide...
And by the rotting staithe,
Where lads come to bathe,
No stir of life is seen
And over the old slips
Where they used to build ships
The grass grows green...

To Keith Mackenzie   The poem by C. Fox Smith
from Ernest H. Shepard   in Punch January 21st
       Sept 1965   1953

99

105
IRREPRESSIBLE HALF:
'NOW THEN, HEEL, CLUB
HE-E-EL!'
HOSTILE VOICE FROM THE
CROWD:
''EEL YERSELF, YER
SLIPPERY LITTLE BLIGHTER'
Signed and inscribed with title
Ink
13 ¾ × 9 ¼ INCHES

106 *(opposite above)*
SHE CHOSE A PINK ONE
Pencil
8 × 6 INCHES
Preliminary drawing for Ernest
Howard Shepard, *Drawn from
Memory*, London: Methuen & Co,
1957, page 120

107 *(opposite below)*
HOW CHRISTMAS
CUSTOMS CAME ABOUT
THESE DITTIES... NOW EXCLUSIVELY
ENLIVEN THE INDUSTRIOUS
SERVANT-MAID
Signed with initials
Inscribed with title below mount
Ink with pencil
4 ½ × 6 INCHES
Illustrated: *Illustrated London News
Christmas Number*, 9 November
1956, page 41

108
HAD ONCE GIVEN HIM
A PENNY
Signed with initials
Inscribed with title below mount
Ink with pencil
6 ½ x 5 INCHES
Illustrated: Ernest Howard
Shepard, *Drawn from Memory*,
London: Methuen & Co, 1957, page 20

FOUGASSE
Cyril Kenneth Bird, CBE (1887-1965)
known as 'Fougasse'

As cartoonist, art editor and editor, Kenneth Bird transformed the style of *Punch*. His own contributions pared down human activity with such economy as to suggest the essence of modern life.

His approach also had a significant influence on poster art for both public information and advertising, as seen here in his work for London Transport [no *109*].

For a biography of Fougasse, please refer to *The Illustrators*, 2009, page 77.

His work is represented in the collections of the London Transport Museum and the V&A.

Further reading:
Bevis Hillier (ed), *Fougasse*, London: Elm Tree Books, 1977; Peter Mellini, 'Bird, (Cyril) Kenneth [pseud. Fougasse] (1887-1965)', H C G Matthew and Brian Harrison (eds), *Oxford Dictionary of National Biography*, Oxford University Press, 2004, vol 5, pages 818-820

109
WE DON'T PLAY GAMES IN THE ROAD
SO WHY DO WE LET OUR CHILDREN?
Inscribed with title
Ink and watercolour
29 x 19 INCHES
Illustrated: Design For a Transport Appeal Poster, circa 1939-1945
Literature: P Herbert (Introduction), *A School of Purposes, A Selection of Fougasse Posters 1939-1945*, London: Methuen & Co, 1946, page 33

$$x = 53 \cdot 5 + 5 \left[\frac{100 W_{P_2O_5}}{W_T} - 18 \right]$$

110
LUNNON TALK
Ink
1 ¾ × 3 ¼ INCHES
Illustrated: *Punch*, 28 July 1954, page 133

Farmers' contributions under the new fertilizer subsidy scheme have been announced by the Ministry of Agriculture, and rural inns are loud with excited comment on the news that the contribution rate is £2 13s 6d a ton for nitro-chalk 'Provided that this amount shall be increased or decreased by five shillings for each one per centum by weight (and proportionately for any fraction thereof) by which the water-soluble phosphoric acid (p205) content is above or below eighteen per centum by weight of the fertilizer.'

111
TAKE A CARBON
Ink
1 ¾ × 3 ¼ INCHES
Illustrated: *Punch*, 2 March 1955, page 275

Good platform phrases don't crop up every day, so Mr Butler's remark about doubling our standard of living has been seized on eagerly by political speakers. already Mr Geoffrey Lloyd, Minister of Fuel and Power, has tried it on a Birmingham audience, and Mr Harold Watkinson, Parliamentary Secretary to the Ministry of Labour, has fired it off successfully at a meeting in Bristol. No one so far has asked what it means however. If it simply means two of everything instead of one, it should be remembered that political speakers will inevitably be included.

112
FRESH AND THRUSTFUL THINKING
Ink
2 × 3 INCHES
Illustrated: *Punch*, 4 December 1957, page 643

Fresh and thrustful thinking on the nation's economic mess was perhaps never more urgently needed than last week, when, fortunately, a grateful public learned that Mr Grimond was condemning high taxation, Mr Gaitskell prescribing expanded production as the cure for inflation, Mr Watkinson asserting that a continued race between wages and prices could ruin us all, and Mr Thorneycroft sponsoring an illustrated booklet advocating stable prices at home and a strong pound abroad.

113
BOUQUET, PLEASE
Ink
2 × 3 ¼ INCHES
Illustrated: *Punch*, 29 June 1955, page 780

A Home Office announcement says that Major Lloyd George has thanked the police for their efforts during the railway strike, and a G.P.O announcement says that the Postmaster-General has thanked the Post Office staff for theirs. It has not yet been decided who is to propose the vote of thanks to the public.

H M BATEMAN
Henry Mayo Bateman (1887-1970)

H M Bateman established his inimitable style before the First World War when, as he put it, he 'went mad on paper', by drawing people's mood and character. This culminated in 'The Man Who ...', his famous series of cartoons dramatising social gaffes.

For a biography of H M Bateman, please refer to *The Illustrators*, 2020, page 56

His work is represented in numerous public collections, including the British Museum.

Further reading:

Anthony Anderson, *The Man Who Was H M Bateman*, Exeter: Webb & Bower, 1982; John Jensen, 'Bateman, Henry Mayo (1887-1970)', H C G Matthew and Brian Harrison (eds), *Oxford Dictionary of National Biography*, Oxford University Press, 2004, vol 4, pages 299-301

114
CARD PLAYERS: 'DIAMONDS'
Signed
Ink and watercolour
9 ½ x 9 INCHES
Exhibited: Langton Gallery,
November 1978, no 37

115
THE DOMINANT SEX
Signed
Inscribed with title below mount
Ink and watercolour
13 × 9 ½ INCHES

116

WIFE (WHO HAS SOMETHING 'ON' HER HUSBAND): 'AND MIND! IF HE BEATS YOU I SHALL DO THE SAME!'
Signed
Inscribed with title below mount
Ink and watercolour
14 ¼ × 10 INCHES
The Tatler, 23 September 1931, page 535;
H M Bateman, *Considered Trifles: A Book of Drawings*, London: Hutchinson & Co, page 33

117

THE INFERIORITY
COMPLEX
Signed and dated 1923
Inscribed with title below mount
Ink and watercolour
14 x 9 ¾ INCHES
Illustrated: *Life*, 29 November 1923
Exhibited: 'Caricatures by H M
Bateman', Leicester Galleries,
London, February-April 1974,
no 75

118
ILLIMITABLE RANGE
Signed
Ink and watercolour
12 ½ x 9 ¼ INCHES

119
THE GIRL WHO THOUGHT SHE WOULD
LIKE A SNAPSHOT OF THE PRINCE
Signed and dated 1922
Ink
14 x 9 ¾ INCHES

120
JUSTIFIABLE PRIDE
Signed
Ink and watercolour
12 ½ x 9 ¼ INCHES

121
WICKET KEEPER: 'HOW'S THAT!'
UMPIRE WITH A GLASS OF GUINNESS:
'VERY REFRESHING!'
Signed
Ink and watercolour
13 x 10 INCHES
Illustrated: Design for an advertisement for Guinness, 1930s

DAVID LOW
Sir David Alexander Cecil Low (1891-1963)

David Low was considered the most outstanding British political cartoonist of his generation. Able to capture recognisable likenesses with great economy, he produced the definitive image of a number of leading figures of the day. And he did so with a subtle combination of ridicule and insight, rather than exaggeration and condemnation. A key feature of his approach was the use of such symbols as the strong but stubborn TUC carthorse and the reactionary Englishman, Colonel Blimp.

David Low was born in Dunedin, New Zealand, on 7 April 1891, the third son of four children of the businessman, David Brown Low, and his wife, Jane (née Flanagan). Educated at the Boys' High School, Christchurch, he made his debut with the Christchurch political weekly, *The Spectator*, at the age of 11 and, in 1908, became the paper's political cartoonist. Later, he moved to the *Canterbury Times* (1910) and then the Sydney weekly, *The Bulletin* (1911). At *The Bulletin*, his technique benefited from the influence of Will Dyson and Norman Lindsay, so that his lampoon of the Australian Prime Minister, William Hughes, entitled *The Billy Book* (1918), proved to be a bestseller.

The success encouraged Low to move to England, in the following year, where he began to work for the *Star*, evening stablemate of the liberal *Daily News*. He established himself with the device of the two-headed Liberal/Tory Coalition Ass. In 1920, he married Madeline Grieve Kenning, of New Zealand. They would have two daughters.

In 1927, Low became political cartoonist for the *Evening Standard* and, though a Socialist, was given full independence on what was a very Conservative publication. This freedom led to the creation, in 1934, of his most famous character, Colonel Blimp, the epitome of British Conservatism. During the 1920s and 30s, he also produced two series of literary and political caricatures for the *New Statesman*. On leaving the *Evening Standard*, he spent a short, unhappy time at the *Daily Herald* (1950-53) where, however, he did produce another of his most controversial images: the TUC cart-horse. With some relief, he was taken on by the *Manchester Guardian* in 1953 and remained there until his death in London on 19 September 1963.

Low's popularity as a newspaper cartoonist created, from very early on, a market for books of caricatures; those published around the period of the Second World War are particularly impressive examples of his incisive criticism. He had total command of his medium, both artistically and intellectually, and was considered the most outstanding British political cartoonist of his generation. This position was officially acknowledged in 1962, when he was knighted.

His work is represented in numerous public collections, including the British Museum, the National Portrait Gallery and the V&A; and the British Cartoon Archive, university of Kent (Canterbury). His papers are in the Beinecke Library (Yale university).

Further reading:

Marguerite Mahood, 'Low, Sir David (Alexander Cecil) (*b* Dunedin, April 7, 1892; *d* London, Sept 20, 1963)', Grove Art Online, 2003, https://doi.org/10.1093/gao/9781884446054.article.T052166;

Colin Seymour-Ure, 'Low, Sir David Alexander Cecil (1891–1963)', H C G Matthew and Brian Harrison (eds), *Oxford Dictionary of National Biography*, Oxford University Press, 2008, https://doi.org/10.1093/ref:odnb/34606;

Colin Seymour-Ure and Jim Schoff, *David Low*, London: Secker & Warburg, 1985

SECRETLY IN THE DEAD OF NIGHT

On 11 December 1936, the day that this cartoon appeared in the *Evening Standard*, King Edward VIII officially abdicated the throne, ending a reign that had lasted just 327 days. Prime Minister Stanley Baldwin had announced the abdication in the Commons the day before. Edward had relinquished the throne in order to marry the American socialite Wallis Simpson, who was in the process of divorcing her second husband. Though it is generally accepted that Edward and Simpson had been lovers since 1934, the affair did not become public through the British press until 2 December 1936, a little over a week before Edward's abdication. Even when the couple spent the summer of 1936 together holidaying in the Mediterranean, an event widely covered in the American and European press, the British press remained silent. On 16 November, Edward met with Stanley Baldwin at Buckingham Palace to inform him of his decision to marry Simpson and was told by the Prime Minister that his marriage to a twice divorcée would be rejected by the government, the country and the Empire, and that the King's public standing would be irrevocably damaged.

When the story broke in the press on 2 December, the King did receive some support for his wishes, not least from Winston Churchill and the press barons, Lord Beaverbrook and Lord Rothermere, who believed Edward had a right to marry whomever he wished. Churchill and Beaverbrook even tried to rally support in Parliament, though only 40 MPs sided with the King. Both the Labour leader, Clement Attlee, and the Archbishop of Canterbury, Cosmo Lang, supported Baldwin's opposition to the marriage. As David Low's cartoon suggests, there was a belief that the King's sudden abdication was driven by the

SECRETLY, IN THE DEAD OF NIGHT.

Prime Minister, Stanley Baldwin, who had so strongly opposed the union and, as was thought, had pressured the King to abdicate. Low's cartoon also suggests that the silence of the British press on the matter until just eight days before the abdication was announced meant that Baldwin was able to press his perceived desire for abdication unencumbered by public opinion, which may have been more sympathetic to the King than the government would have hoped.

122
SECRETLY, IN THE DEAD
OF NIGHT
Signed and inscribed with title
Ink and pencil
12 ¼ × 18 ¾ INCHES
Illustrated: *Evening Standard*,
11 December 1936

APPLICANTS FOR THE JOB

In March 1936, Prime Minister Stanley Baldwin's National Government appointed the first Minister for Co-ordination of Defence, a position established in response to criticism that Britain's armed forces were under-strength in comparison to Nazi Germany. A vocal critic of Baldwin's perceived reluctance towards rearmament was Winston Churchill, and many expected him to be appointed to the position to oversee the process. In the end, on 13 March 1936, Baldwin named Sir Thomas Inskip as the new Minister, a politician with an exclusively legal track record and no experience of military matters. An unknown source at the time was quoted as calling it 'the most cynical appointment since Caligula made his horse a consul'.

Published a little over a week before the new Minister for Co-Ordination of Defence was announced, Sir David Low's cartoon appeared at a time of much speculation amongst journalists and commentators over who would be chosen for the role. The cartoon suggests a concern felt by a British public that largely supported a policy of pacifism, that certain figures in the Government would use the role and the policy of rearmament for more aggressive means, rather than for support of the League of Nations as Stanley Baldwin had indicated. David Low suggests a queue of ideal 'applicants for the job' based on their pacifist leanings.

Appearing in the cartoon are:

The writer **H G Wells** (1866-1946), best known for works including *The Time Machine* (1895) and *The War of the Worlds* (1898). Recognised through much of his career for his pacifist views – he referred to himself as 'an extreme pacifist' in his 1917 work *War and the Future* – he later became a staunch supporter of military action against Germany in both the First World War and following the rise of Nazi Germany. This is perhaps suggested by Wells looking as if he has failed in his interview.

Lord Robert Cecil (1864-1958) was one of the architects of the foundation of the League of Nations, set up in 1920 with the principal mission to maintain world peace. He worked throughout the 1930s to promote disarmament in Europe despite the growing threat of Nazi Germany. In 1937, he was awarded the Nobel Peace Prize.

A scholar and an intellectual, **Gilbert Murray** (1866-1957) was a well-known humanist and served as president of the Ethical Union (now Humanists UK) from 1929 to 1930. Though he did not consider himself a pacifist, he was a leader of the League of Nations Society and the League of Nations Union, which campaigned for an international organisation of nations with the aim of preventing war.

Norman Angell (1872-1967) was one of the principal founders of the Union of Democratic Control, a pressure group formed in 1914 to press for a more responsive foreign policy and opposed to military influence in government. He was an executive for the World Committee against War and Fascism from 1933, the year he was awarded the Nobel Peace Prize.

As a philosopher and writer of influential works such as *Brave New World* (1932), **Aldous Huxley** (1894-1963) was known during this period for his writings on pacifist themes. These works included *Eyeless in Gaza* (1936), *Ends and Means* (1937) and *An Encyclopaedia of Pacifism* (1937). He was also a prominent member of the Peace Pledge Union, Britain's leading pacifist organisation.

Most famous as the author of the *Winnie-the-Pooh* collection of children's stories, **A A Milne** (1882-1956) had been a pacifist in the lead up to the First World War, but enlisted voluntarily and saw action on the Western Front. The horrors he witnessed strengthened his anti-war stance, and in 1934 he wrote *Peace with Honour*, a pacifist denunciation of war.

C E M Joad (1891-1953) was a philosopher and broadcaster who had become a well-known figure in society through his popularising of philosophy, publishing first *Guide to Modern Thought* (1933) and then *Guide to Philosophy* (1936). He had been an outspoken proponent of pacifism before the First World War and in the 1930s, despite being a strong opponent of Nazism, was also firmly against militarism and rearmament. During this period he became a supporter of pacifist organisations such as the No More War Movement and the Peace Pledge Union.

Philip Noel-Baker (1889-1982), was also closely involved in the formation of the League of Nations, serving as Lord Cecil's assistant and working himself as a renowned campaigner for disarmament. He also served as assistant to the Foreign Secretary Arthur Henderson whilst he was President of the World Disarmament Conference in Geneva in 1932 to 1933. A talented athlete in his youth, Philip Noel-Baker represented Britain in the 800m and 1500m at the 1912 Olympics in Stockholm and the 1920 Olympics in Antwerp, winning a silver medal in the 1500m at the latter.

Styled as the 'Superintendent of Golders Green Fire Brigade', bringing up the rear in the queue to be interviewed is **Sir David Low** himself. Though he was strongly against appeasement in the face of Europe's dictators, his presence here suggests a belief that he trusted his own convictions more than those in the running for the role.

123 (opposite)
APPLICANTS FOR THE JOB
Signed and inscribed with title
Ink with pencil
12 ½ × 18 ½ INCHES
Illustrated: *Evening Standard*, 6 March 1936

Baldwin may say that this arms programme is for support of the League, but there's no guarantee that his hard-boiled diehards will not collar the finished war machine and use it in an opposite direction. Now it would be reassuring if the job of Defence Minister could be entrusted to one of us competent pacifists.....

SITUATION VACANT

WAR-LORD Wanted. Excellent wages, uniform provided, good outings, use of car. APPLY WITHIN

APPLICANTS FOR THE JOB.

EASTON GLEBE, DUNMOW.

124 (detail)
H G WELLS
Drawn on headed letter paper: Easton Glebe, Dunmow
Pencil
8 × 6 INCHES
Illustrated: Preliminary drawing for *The New Statesman*

H G Wells, rented Easton Glebe in Dunmow from 1910-1928 and it was during this time that Wells had a 10 year affair with Rebecca West. Easton Glebe was on the Easton Lodge estate which belonged to his friend and fellow socialist the Countess of Warwick.

PONT

Graham Laidler, ARIBA (1908-1940), known as 'Pont'

Following in the *Punch* tradition of George Du Maurier and Frank Reynolds, Graham 'Pont' Laidler excelled at satirising the British middle classes. Before his premature death at the age of just 32, Laidler had established a reputation as one of the finest cartoonists of the twentieth century with his acute observations of 'the British Character'.

For a biography of Pont, please refer to *The Illustrators*, 2014, page 130

125

IT OCCURS TO ME, JOSEPHINE DEAR, THAT YOU MIGHT HAVE LEFT SOMETHING IN THE OVEN
Signed
Inscribed with title below mount
Ink
8 x 11 ½ INCHES
Provenance: The Victoria Wood Collection
Illustrated: Pont, *Most of Us Are Absurd*, London: Collins, 1946, page 88

126

WE MUST ON NO ACCOUNT PERMIT ANYONE TO GIVE US A SHOCK, MR PEMBRIDGE. THE LEAST SHOCK OF ANY SORT WOULD, IN OUR PRESENT STATE OF HEALTH, BE SURE TO KILL US IMMEDIATELY
Signed
Ink
10 ½ x 9 INCHES
Illustrated: *Punch*, 21 October 1936, page 461

127
I ONLY JUST SAW IT IN
TIME, BY JOVE!
Signed
Ink
12 ¾ × 10 INCHES
Illustrated: *Punch*, 21 November
1934, page 579

128

THE BRITISH CHARACTER

LOVE OF DUMB ANIMALS

Signed

Ink

7 x 10 ½ INCHES

Illustrated: *Punch*, 10 October 1934, page 396;

Pont, *The British Character*, London: Collins, 1938, page 50

Edward Ardizzone

EDWARD ARDIZZONE

EDWARD ARDIZZONE
Edward Ardizzone, CBE RA RDI (1900-1979)

Highly observant and immensely humane, the work of Edward Ardizzone is in direct descent from the finest French and English illustrators of the nineteenth century. Developing as an artist from 1930, Ardizzone made his name as an illustrator through his contributions to *The Radio Times* and then with *Little Tim* and the *Brave Sea Captain*, which proved to be one of the most significant picture books published between the wars. Soon considered one of the greatest illustrators of his generation, he also gained a reputation as an Official War Artist. Versatile and productive, he produced paintings, sculptures, etchings and lithographs, and worked as a designer.

For a biography of Edward Ardizzone, please refer to *The Illustrators*, 2019, page 79.

Paul Cox has drawn a personal homage to Edward Ardizzone and the Maida Vale pubs that he both frequented and illustrated in Maurice Gorman's *The Local* and *Back to the Local*, (1939 and 1949). Ardizzone's illustrations proved to be a valuable social record of post-war pub culture, capturing the quintessential characters and architecture of a London suburb. Please see chapter 15, pages 233-240

SELF-PORTRAIT,
CIRCA 1929
Oil on canvas
19 x 14 ½ INCHES
Provenance: Artist's family by descent:
Private Collection
Exhibited: 'Edward Ardizzone RA 1900-1979: A Centenary Celebration', Ashmolean Museum, Oxford, September-November 2000, no 34;

'This depicts Ardizzone in his late twenties at the beginning of his career as an artist. Remembered by most as jolly, rotund and bald, this is a rare representation of him with a full head of hair and relatively slim.'
(*Edward Ardizzone RA 1900-1979: A Centenary Celebration*, Oxford: Ashmolean Museum, 2000, [unpaginated])

129 (opposite)
THE BAR MAID
Signed with initials
Watercolour, bodycolour and pencil
7 x 8 ½ INCHES

NURSE MATILDA

by Christianna Brand

Christianna Brand was the pseudonym of Mary Christianna Milne (1907-1988), best known for her series of novels featuring detective Inspector Cockrill, and for the *Nurse Matilda* series of books for children, which were illustrated by her cousin Edward Ardizzone.

Later made into the Nanny McPhee films starring Emma Thomson, the Nurse Matilda books feature the hideously ugly Nurse Matilda, who is employed as a governess by Mr Brown to manage his many and very naughty children. Nurse Matilda uses her magic and forcible personality to teach the children how to behave. Christianna Brand wrote two sequels; *Nurse Matilda Goes to Town* and *Nurse Matilda Goes to Hospital.*

Nos *130–146* are all executed in ink and are illustrated in Christianna Brand, *Nurse Matilda*, Leicester: Brockhampton Press, 1964

130

MRS BROWN WAS VERY SWEET AND SHE NEVER COULD BELIEVE THAT THE CHILDREN WERE REALLY NAUGHTY. SHE OPENED HER EYES WIDE AND SAID, 'OH DEAR, WHAT HAVE THEY BEEN DOING NOW?'

10 ¾ × 7 INCHES
Illustrated: page 8

131

NURSE MATILDA

3 ¾ x 5 INCHES
Illustrated: facing title page

132
'GOOD EVENING, MR AND MRS
BROWN, I AM NURSE MATILDA.'

8 x 5 ¼ INCHES
Illustrated: page 15

133
NURSE MATILDA LOOKED THEM ALL OVER QUIETLY WITH HER BLACK, BEADY
EYES; AND THEN SHE THUMPED ONCE MORE ON THE FLOOR WITH HER STICK.

5 x 6 INCHES
Illustrated: page 23

134

THEIR HANDS SEIZED UP THEIR SPOONS AND DOWN WENT THE PORRIDGE,
STUFF, STUFF, STODGE, STODGE, ON TOP OF ALL THAT BREAD AND BUTTER.

4 ¾ × 6 ½ INCHES
Illustrated: page 30

135

THE CHILDREN PUFFED
AND BLEW, THEIR CHEEKS
BULGED, THEIR EYES
GOGGLED.

2 × 4 INCHES
Illustrated: page 31

136

WHEN NURSE MATILDA WENT UP TO
THE SCHOOLROOM TO BEGIN THE FIRST
MORNING'S LESSON, THE CHILDREN
WERE SITTING ALL AROUND THE HUGE
TABLE AS GOOD AS GOLD

.

4 ½ × 4 INCHES
Illustrated: page 33

137
'OH DEAR, I THINK THE DOGS NEED TO BE LET OUT,' AND
BENT DOWN AND TOOK THEM BY THE SCRUFFS OF THEIR
PINAFORES AND LED THEM TO THE DOOR AND DOWN
THE STAIRS AND INTO THE GARDEN: AND PUSHED THEM
OUTSIDE AND CLOSED THE GARDEN DOOR ON THEM.

6 ½ x 6 ¼ INCHES
Illustrated: page 35

138
IF THEY WRIGGLED; AND IF THEY TIPPED BACKWARDS
ONLY JUST THE LITTLEST BIT, THE WHOLE CHAIR WENT
OVER WITH A CRASH AND LANDED THEM ON THE FLOOR
WITH THEIR LEGS IN THE AIR – AND THERE THEY STUCK!

5 ¼ x 7 INCHES
Illustrated: page 37

139

NEXT MORNING THE CHILDREN WOULDN'T GET UP

4 x 4 INCHES
Illustrated: page 38

140

YOU NEEDN'T THINK THAT FROM THEN ON THE
BROWN CHILDREN WERE ALWAYS GOOD – INDEED
THEY WEREN'T!

4 x 3 ¾ INCHES
Illustrated: page 48

141
AND IN THAT VERY INSTANT, OUT OF THE KITCHEN, HELMETED IN SAUCE-PANS,
HUNG ABOUT WITH BAKING-TINS, ARMED WITH FRYING-PANS AND ROLLING-
PINS AND BROOMS AND MOPS AND FLAT-IRONS AND A HUGE PAIR OF CURLING
TONGS DASHED HOPPITT AND COOK ...

4 x 6 ½ INCHES
Illustrated: page 57

142

BY THE TIME THE OTHER VILLAGE CHILDREN ARRIVED, THE BROWNS WERE
ALL LOLLING ABOUT RUBBING THEIR STOMACHS AND CRYING OUT, 'OW!
OW! OW!' ...
'WE WERE WARNED NEVER TO EAT BOY,' SAID THE BROWNS, 'AND NOW
WE HAVE AND THE GROWN-UPS WERE QUITE RIGHT: HE'S GIVEN US
AWFUL PAINS,'

5 ¼ × 6 INCHES
Illustrated: page 73

143

SHE HAD BEEN THINKING THIS OVER,
SHE SAID, AND HAD COME TO THE
CONCLUSION THAT MR AND MRS
BROWN HAD TOO MANY CHILDREN

6 ¼ × 4 ½ INCHES
Illustrated: page 84

144

IN THE DRAWING-ROOM, CONSTABLE FIGGS HAD EXPLAINED MATTERS AND MR
BROWN HAD GONE UP TO THE NURSERY TO SUMMON THE CHILDREN. THEY FILED IN
AND STOOD IN A RING ON THE DRAWING-ROOM CARPET.
'IT 'AS BEEN REPORTED TO ME,' SAID CONSTABLE FIGGS, LOOKING DOWN AT THEM
REPROACHFULLY, 'THAT YOU'VE ATE UP THAT YOUNG GREEN; HAD 'IM FOR YOUR
DINNER?'

4 ¼ x 5 ½ INCHES
Illustrated: page 77

145
NOW THEY WERE REALLY RUNNING AWAY AND THERE WAS NOTHING TO BE DONE ABOUT IT BUT JUST TO KEEP ON.

1 ½ x 3 ¼ INCHES
Illustrated: page 108

146
AND AT THAT MOMENT, JUST AS THEY WERE THINKING IT – COULDN'T HELP THINKING IT – SHE GAVE ONE LAST THUMP WITH HER STICK ON THE GROUND AND – WHAT DO YOU THINK HAPPENED? THAT TOOTH OF HERS FLEW OUT, AND LANDED ON THE FLOOR AT THE CHILDREN'S FEET. AND IT BEGAN TO GROW ...

4 ¼ x 6 INCHES
Illustrated: page 127

Postwar Illustrators & Cartoonists

POSTWAR ILLUSTRATORS & CARTOONISTS

ROWLAND EMETT
Frederick Rowland Emett, OBE (1906-1990)

Rowland Emett established himself as the creator of elegant and whimsical cartoons during the 1930s, while working as an industrial draughtsman. In 1951, he reached a wider public with his designs for The Far Tottering and Oyster Creek Railway, which was sited at Battersea Park during the Festival of Britain. Gradually, he converted more of his illustrations into increasingly complex three-dimensional machines. Both drawings and inventions helped cheer a nation fed up with years of austerity.

For a biography of Rowland Emett, please refer to *The Illustrators*, 2019, page 105.

147
A HARROWING PROSPECT OF MOUNT PLEASANT
Signed and inscribed with title and further extensively inscribed
Ink and watercolour; 17 ½ × 25 INCHES

MERVYN PEAKE

Mervyn Peake (1911-1968)

Though already developing as a painter, Mervyn Peake established himself as a writer and illustrator in 1939, with *Captain Slaughterboard Drops Anchor*, a comic fantasy intended for children. This revealed that he had an outstanding talent for the grotesque, and was ready to align himself to Romantic tendencies in British art. He applied that talent to a broad range of visual and verbal forms, central to which was his 'Gormenghast' trilogy, an extraordinary imaginative achievement detailing a parallel world.

His work is represented in numerous public collections, including the Imperial War Museum; and the Wordsworth Trust (Grasmere). The Mervyn Peake Archive, which includes original drawings, is held by the British Library.

Further reading:

John Batchelor, *Mervyn Peake. a biographical and critical exploration*, London: Duckworth, 1974;

Colin Manlove (rev Clare L Taylor), 'Peake, Mervyn Laurence (1911-1968)', in H C G Matthew and Brian Harrison (eds), *Oxford Dictionary of National Biography*, Oxford University Press, 2004, vol 43, pages 269-271;

John Watney, *Mervyn Peake*, London: Michael Joseph, 1976;

G Peter Winnington (ed), *Mervyn Peake. The Man and His Art*, London: Peter Owen Publishers, 2006;

G Peter Winnington, *Vast Alchemies. The Life and Work of Mervyn Peake*, London: Peter Owen Publishers, 2000;

Malcolm Yorke, *Mervyn Peake: My Eyes Mint Gold: A Life*, London: John Murray, 2000

UNCLE GEORGE

Uncle George became so Nosey
That we bought him a Tea-Cosy

To defend ourselves, and bring
Confusion to the evil thing;

Which angered him so much, we had
To tie him to a blotting pad

Which soaks his energy away
From dawn to dusk, and dusk to day,

Until he's now so out of joint
That he can never see the Point.

148

UNCLE GEORGE
Inscribed with title and poem on separate sheet
Ink
10 × 8 ½ INCHES

IONICUS

Joshua Charles Armitage (1913-1998), known as 'Ionicus'

Working as 'Ionicus', Joshua Charles Armitage is probably best remembered for the covers that he produced for a Penguin paperback edition of the books of P G Wodehouse and for the many cartoons that he contributed to *Punch*. However, he was a varied and prolific illustrator, cartoonist and painter who has been admired for his craftsmanship and clarity of vision.

Joshua Charles Armitage was born in the coastal town of Hoylake, Cheshire, on 26 September 1913, the son of the fisherman, Joshua Armitage, and his wife (Kate) Louise (née Cooke). At the time of his birth the family was living at 42 Groveland Avenue, Hoylake, and it would remain his home until his marriage.

In 1929, a Cheshire County Art Scholarship enabled Armitage to study at Liverpool City School of Art, where his teachers included Will Penn. On completing the course in 1935, he worked as an art teacher in junior instruction, and also began to show work at the exhibitions of the Liverpool Academy of Arts. In 1939, he married Catherine Buckle, and they initially lived with her mother at 31 Marmion Road, Hoylake. They would have two daughters.

During the Second World War, Armitage served in the Royal Navy, though problems with his eyesight prevented him from obtaining a commission. After a spell working on minesweepers, he spent most of the war as a gunnery instructor in Liverpool. Nevertheless, he continued to develop as an artist, producing a design for a mural for a naval canteen, which became the first of his two exhibits at the Royal Academy of Arts (1943 & 1945), and other naval subjects, shown at the Royal Cambrian Academy of Art, Conway (also 1943 & 1945). He also contributed cartoons to the Admiralty sponsored monthly, *The Ditty Box: The Navy's Own Magazine*, and was still in service when he began to submit them to *Punch*. The first appeared on 29 March 1944. It was the Ionic columns that appeared in its background that gave Armitage the idea of using 'Ionicus' as his pseudonym.

Following demobilisation, Armitage returned to teaching art, while continuing to contribute to *Punch*, in an association that would last over 40 years, and yield more than 350 drawings. His final teaching position was as an instructor at Wallasey School of Art in the years 1948-50, and from 1950 he worked full-time as a freelance artist. The many periodicals for which he worked include *Amateur Gardening*, *Dalesman* (covers for 17 years), *Lilliput*, *Radio Times*, the *Financial Times* and *Tatler*. He also produced advertisements, including images of stately homes and coaching inns for Martins Bank that he drew in the early 1950s.

In the late 1940s, Armitage began to illustrate a wide range of books, the earliest of which was probably Geoffrey Lowis's *Ruthless Roger's School for Pirates* (1948). He worked on nearly 400 books in all, either as illustrator or

cover designer, and developed long associations with several publishers, notably Chatto & Windus, Dent, Hodder & Stoughton, William Kimber, Macmillan, Oxford University Press and Penguin Books. He designed covers for the last of these from 1968, including 58 for titles by P G Wodehouse, which probably became his most famous achievement as an illustrator.

A member of the Royal Liverpool Golfing Club, Armitage produced many watercolours of golfing subjects, including a set that was reproduced in 1971 and issued in a portfolio entitled *100th Open Championship at Royal Birkdale*. He was also commissioned to produce 12 watercolours for the Oxford and Cambridge Club in London.

Continuing to live in Hoylake throughout his life, including many years at 34 Avondale Road, Armitage became President of the local Deeside Art Group. He died on 29 January 1998, surviving his wife by a decade.

His work is represented in the collections of the British Cartoon Archive (University of Kent, Canterbury).

149

THE GOLDMAKER'S HOUSE, FRONT AND BACK COVER
Signed
Ink and watercolour
9 × 12 ¼ INCHES
Illustrated: Iirmelin Sandman Lilius, *The Goldmaker's House*, Oxford University Press, 1977, cover

Stamped on reverse with J.C. Armitage (Ionicus), 34 Avondale Road, Hoylake, Cheshire, 051-632-1298

150
THE BRASS BOTTLE
Signed
Ink
5 × 4 ¾ INCHES
Illustrated: *Radio Times*, 5 April 1954

151
... WHO WOULDN'T EAT HIS PORRIDGE
Signed
Ink
2 × 6 ½ INCHES
Illustrated: *Radio Times*, 23 November 1956

RONALD SEARLE

Ronald William Fordham Searle, CBE (1920-2011)

Equally inspired by a wide range of experience and a great knowledge of the history of caricature, Ronald Searle honed an incisive graphic skill to develop an unparalleled graphic oeuvre, an oeuvre that has made him one of the most popular and influential cartoonist-illustrators.

For a biography of Ronald Searle, please refer to *The Illustrators*, 2018, page 94.

For essays on various aspects of Ronald Searle's achievement, see *The Illustrators*, 1999, pages 228-230; and *The Illustrators*, 2000, pages 40-42.

Chris Beetles Gallery published Russell Davies's *Ronald Searle*. In the 2003 edition of the 1990 biography, Russell Davies and Ronald Searle added corrections and brought up to date the exhibitions list and bibliography.

Chris Beetles Gallery also held the major tribute exhibition, 'Ronald Searle Remembered', in May-June 2012. It was accompanied by a 200 page fully illustrated paperback catalogue, containing newly researched essays and notes.

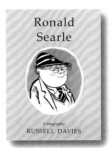

152
PSST! WANNA BUY SOME SULPHUR?
Signed, inscribed with title and dated 1951
Ink
12 × 5 ¾ INCHES
Illustrated: *Sunday Express*, 22 April 1951

153
MIDSUMMER MADNESS
Ink and watercolour
54 ¾ x 45 INCHES

On loan from a Private Collection

154 *(opposite)*
CAT TAKING TEA
Signed and dated 1993
Ink and watercolour with pencil
15 ¾ x 16 ½ INCHES

155
PETS
Signed
Ink and watercolour
15 ¾ × 12 ½ INCHES

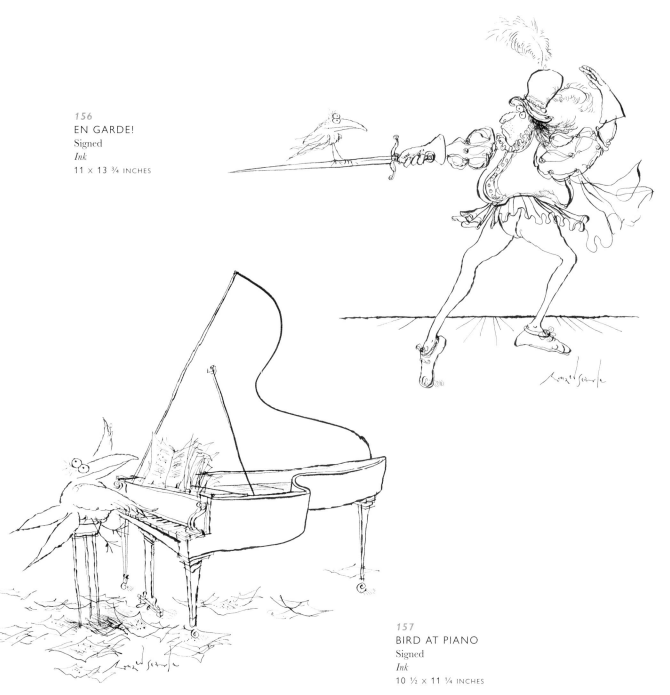

156
EN GARDE!
Signed
Ink
11 x 13 ¾ INCHES

157
BIRD AT PIANO
Signed
Ink
10 ½ x 11 ¼ INCHES

Punch issue May 18
[Ross]
Lawrence of Arabia } ALEC GUINNESS
Aircraftman Ross
(Haymarket Theatre)

Ronald Searle

158
LAWRENCE OF ARABIA,
AIRCRAFTMAN ROSS: –
ALEC GUINNESS
Signed and inscribed with title
and '*Punch*, issue May 18',
'[Ross]' and '(Haymarket
Theatre)'
Ink
18 × 15 INCHES
Illustrated: *Punch*, 18 May 1960

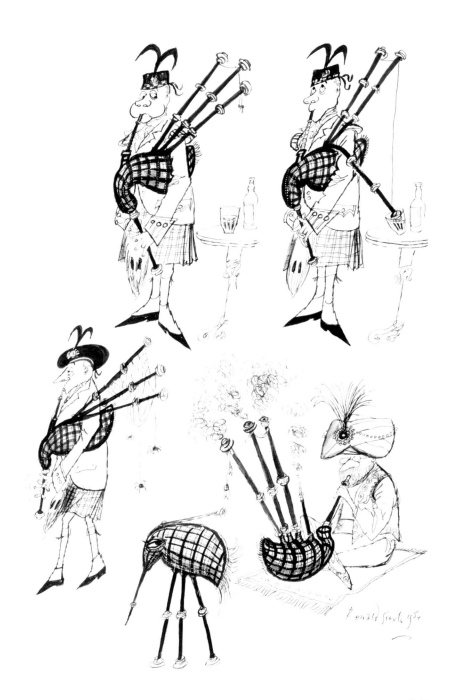

159

THE PIPES! THE PIPES!
THE EDINBURGH
INTERNATIONAL FESTIVAL
OF DRAMA OPENS
TOMORROW
Signed, inscribed with title, and
'*News Chronicle*, Saturday cartoon
issue, August 21', and dated 1954
Ink
21 ½ × 14 ¼ INCHES
Provenance: Peter & Pat Crofts
Collection
Illustrated: *News Chronicle*, London
Literature: Ronald Searle,
Merry England, Perpetua Books:
London, 1956, pages 106-107

160
THE GREEN SWARD
Signed, inscribed with title and dated 1954
Ink and watercolour
22 × 15 ¼ INCHES
Illustrated: *News Chronicle*, London, 24 July 1954
'Saturday Sketchbook';
Merry England, Etc, London: Perpetua Books,
1956, pages 58 and 59

NORMAN THELWELL

Norman Thelwell (1923-2004)

Norman Thelwell is arguably the most popular cartoonist to have worked in Britain since the Second World War. Though almost synonymous with his immortal subject of little girls and their fat ponies, his work is far more wide ranging, perceptive – and indeed prescient – than that association suggests.

For a biography of Norman Thelwell, please refer to *The Illustrators*, 2020, page 154.

Further reading:
Mark Bryant, 'Thelwell, Norman (1923-2004)', H C G Matthew and Brian Harrison (eds), *Oxford Dictionary of National Biography*, Oxford University Press, 2008, https://doi.org/10.1093/ref:odnb/93356

Having mounted major exhibitions of the work of Thelwell in 1989 and 1991, Chris Beetles encouraged further interest in the artist in 2009 with 'The Definitive Thelwell' and its accompanying catalogue. The 100-page catalogue surveys all aspects of his career, through 177 illustrations, an appreciation, a biographical chronology and a full bibliography.

Nos *161* & *162* were produced as part of a marketing campaign for Biorex Laboratories Ltd. Biorex were developers of a cream called Biosone GA, which was similar to hydrocortisone cream.

161
AN ITCH FOR LIQUORICE
Signed
Ink and watercolour
7 ¾ x 10 ¾ INCHES

162
SPACE AGE ITCH
Signed
Ink and watercolour with bodycolour
9 ½ x 13 ¼ INCHES

163

I RESOLVE TO BE A GOOD BOY

Signed and inscribed with title

Ink with bodycolour

3 ½ x 5 ½ INCHES

Illustrated: Preliminary drawing for *Belt Up: Thelwell's Motoring Manual*, London: Eyre Methuen, 1974, page 60

Exhibited: 'Thelwell: Huntin', Shootin', Fishin', Sailin', Farmin', Golfin', Gardenin' ...', Chris Beetles Gallery, London, September 1990

164

THE HORSE IS MAN'S BEST FRIEND

Ink

2 ½ x 9 INCHES

Illustrated: Norman Thelwell, *Penelope Rides Again*, London: Methuen, 1989

Exhibited: 'Norman Thelwell: Huntin', Shootin', Fishin', Sailin', Farmin', Golfin', Gardenin'...', Chris Beetles Gallery, London, September 1990

165

YOU DON'T CARE A DAMN WHAT
I LOOK LIKE
Signed and inscribed with title
Ink
5 ¼ × 6 INCHES
Exhibited: 'Norman Thelwell: Huntin', Shootin',
Fishin', Sailin', Farmin', Golfin', Gardenin'...',
Chris Beetles Gallery, London, September 1990

166

IF THE FARMER SEES ALL THE LITTER
WE'VE DROPPED – HE'LL BE LIVID!
Signed and inscribed with title
Ink and watercolour
7 × 9 INCHES
Exhibited: 'Norman Thelwell: Huntin', Shootin',
Fishin', Sailin', Farmin', Golfin', Gardenin'...',
Chris Beetles Gallery, London, September 1990

CHARLES KEEPING

Charles William James Keeping (1924-1988)

As an illustrator and lithographer, Charles Keeping produced dynamic and emotive images. He became particularly well known for his work on historical novels for children, and produced the first full edition of Dickens to be illustrated by a single artist. He also wrote the texts to his own highly memorable picture books.

Charles Keeping was born in Lambeth, East London, on 22 September 1924. His secure and happy upbringing had an unusually important effect in shaping both the man and the artist. In spending his childhood in a house that overlooked an active stable yard, he became a frequent and accurate observer of horses and carts. While, in working as a gas meter rent collector in areas of poverty, he gained the experience that made him the perfect modern artist to illustrate the work of Charles Dickens.

Keeping attended the Frank Bryant School for Boys, in Kennington, leaving at the age of 14 to become apprenticed to a printer. On the outbreak of the Second World War, he was conscripted into the Royal Navy. When the war was over, he studied art at the Regent Street Polytechnic (1946-52), where he met the designer and illustrator Renate Meyer, whom he later married. He took various jobs, including cartoonist on the *Daily Herald*, before starting working as a book illustrator. In 1956, he was commissioned by the Oxford University Press to illustrate stories for children written by Rosemary Sutcliffe, and with the encouragement of the doyenne of children's book editors, Mabel George of OUP, was launched on a career which for three decades made him one of the best known and more prolific illustrators (1960-1980s). He made brilliant use of colour and the new printing techniques, using a mixture of gouache, tempera, watercolour and inks. He was an early enthusiast for Plasticowell, the grained plastic sheets designed by the printers, Cowells of Ipswich, for lithographic illustrations.

Keeping won the Kate Greenaway award for *Charley, Charlotte and the Golden Canary* (1967), and again for *The Highwayman* (1981); he was a prize-winner in the Francis Williams Award for *Tinker, Tailor* (1968), and for Kevin Crossley-Holland's *The Wildman* (1976); and he won the Emil Award for 1987 for *Jack the Treacle Eater*. His commitment to the immense project to illustrate the complete Dickens for the Folio Society was total, and he completed it just before his death on 16 May 1988.

Further reading:
Douglas Martin, *Charles Keeping: an illustrator's life*, London: Julia Macrae Books, 1993

167

IT'S A LONG, LONG WAY TO TIPPERARY

Signed and dated 74
Ink and pencil; 4 × 9 ½ INCHES
Illustrated: Charles Keeping, *Cockney Ding Dong. A Song Book*, Harmondsworth: Kestral Books/EMI Music Publishing, 1975, page 169

Growing up in Kennington and Vauxhall, Charles Keeping and his large, extended family would frequently have a Saturday night 'ding dong' (cockney rhyming slang for 'song'), where they would sing around the piano, drink, eat and be merry. Wishing to record and preserve the songs he grew up with, he produced a fully illustrated book of song and sheet music. *Cockney Ding Dong* was published in 1975 by Kestrel Books, in collaboration with EMI music publishing.

168
COCKNEY DING DONG
Signed and dated 74
Inscribed 'Altogether Songs' and
'159' below mount
Ink
11 ½ × 8 ¾ INCHES
Illustrated: Charles Keeping,
Cockney Ding Dong, Harmondsworth:
Kestral Books/ EMI Publishing,
1975, page 159, 'Altogether Songs'

LARRY

Terence Parkes (1927-2003), known as 'Larry'

Larry was the cartoonist's cartoonist, highly respected by his peers for his consistently funny work, and cherished by them for his affability. In the autobiographical *Larry on Larry, My Life in Cartoons* (1994), he wrote, 'I seem to have the reputation for a being a beer-swigging Brummie cartoonist', and while each particular of that statement may have been true, its overall spirit suggests an essential modesty. He even expressed some reservations about the increasing seriousness with which cartooning was being taken, and yet was steeped in the history of his profession and, more widely, in the history of art. This combination of the easygoing and the erudite informed much of his work, in content and draughtsmanship, and he will long be remembered for both his frequent depiction of an Everyman figure, 'Larry's man', and his parodies of famous works of art.

For a biography of Larry, please refer to *The Illustrators*, 2014, page 226.

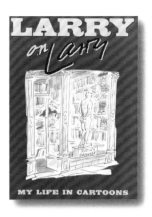

Published in 1994, *Larry on Larry, My Life in Cartoons* is an autobiography of the man known as the cartoonist's cartoonist, told through his work.

169
GETAWAY
BOBSLEIGH
Signed
Ink and watercolour
9 ½ x 13 ½ INCHES

170 (left)
HERR HITLER GOING TO HIS RINGSIDE SEAT IN THE OLYMPICS BOXING STADIUM. BERLIN 1936
Signed and inscribed with title
Ink and watercolour
9 ¼ x 14 ¼ INCHES

171 (below left)
VIVALDI – THE FOOTBALL SEASON
Signed
Watercolour
9 ¾ x 14 INCHES

172 (below right)
ELECTION FEVER
Signed
Ink and watercolour
9 ½ x 10 ½ INCHES

173 (right)
A DIFFICULT LIE
BY GRAHAM SUTHERLAND
Signed
Ink
6 ¼ × 6 INCHES

174 (below left)
GLASGOW SCHOOL
Signed
Ink
6 × 5 ¾ INCHES

175 (below right)
RODIN'S JACK RUSSELL
Signed
Ink
5 ¾ × 6 INCHES

JOHN BURNINGHAM
John Mackintosh Burningham (1936-2019)

John Burningham was arguably the greatest British creator of picture books since the Second World War, with an oeuvre that ranges from *Borka* (1963) through *Mr Gumpy's Outing* (1970) to late achievements that include *Motor Miles* (2015) and *Mouse House* (2017). Popular with all ages, he sometimes aimed a subject particularly at adults, as with *John Burningham's Champagne* (2015).

For a biography of John Burningham, please refer to *The Illustrators*, 2018, page 117.

In December 2016, the Chris Beetles Gallery mounted its own major selling retrospective of work by John Burningham. It was accompanied by a fully-illustrated 88-page catalogue, containing an appreciative essay, a chronology and a comprehensive bibliography.

John Burningham
An illustrator for all ages

176
BORKA WAS SOON VERY FRIENDLY WITH THE CAPTAIN, FRED AND OF COURSE WITH FOWLER
Bodycolour with ink and elements of collage
16 ½ x 25 ½ inches
Illustrated: John Burningham, *Borka: The Adventures of a Goose with No Feathers*, London: Jonathan Cape, 1963, [unpaginated]

William Scully

WILLIAM  SCULLY

WILLIAM SCULLY
William Scully (1917-2002)

During a career that spanned almost 60 years, William Scully forged a reputation as one of the most prolific and widely published cartoonists of the twentieth century. His loose but carefully considered cartoons were quintessentially British in their humour, but with a style and wit that could stand comparison with the great cartoonists of *The New Yorker*. His editor at *Punch*, William Hewison, described his work as 'Marvellously free and autographic but with a tight control over the use of tone. You are always aware of space in a Scully drawing.'

William Scully was born on 12 June 1917 in Ilkeston, Derbyshire, the son of a builder and amateur artist. After graduating from Nottingham School of Art, he worked as a pipe-tester at an ironworks for four years and then for seven years in an artificial silk factory, before having his first cartoons accepted by the *Bystander*. During the Second World War, he served in the Army Ordnance Corps, also becoming Art Editor of the army magazine *AIM* from 1943 to 1945. Between 1945 and 1946, he worked on the staff of the magazine *Soldier*, set up by James Friell, the political cartoonist of *The Daily Worker* who worked under the pseudonym 'Gabriel'.

For almost 60 years, William Scully's cartoons appeared weekly in publications including *Punch*, *Spectator*, *Sketch*, *London Opinion*, *Men Only*, *Lilliput* and *Tatler* as well as in the *New Yorker*. For many years, 'Scully's View' appeared in the *Sunday Telegraph*. His cartoons were still being published until only weeks before his death in November 2002, at the age of 85.

177

AH, DR GILBY, SO YOU TOOK MRS CURRIE'S ADVICE
Signed and inscribed with title
Ink, watercolour and bodycolour
13 x 9 INCHES
Illustrated: *Punch*, December 1988, cover

178 (above)

ALSO A QUALIFIED QUACK, I SEE
Signed and inscribed with title
Ink and watercolour
9 ¼ × 8 INCHES

179 (above right)

YOU'RE PRETTY TOUGH AND RESILIENT. I'M SURE YOU'LL
STAND UP TO THE HAZARDS OF HOSPITAL TREATMENT
Signed and inscribed with title
Ink and watercolour
9 × 7 INCHES

180 (right)

THAT WAS YOUR OFFICE, EXPRESSING THEIR CONCERN
AND SYMPATHY – FOR ME, THAT IS
Signed and inscribed with title
Ink and watercolour
10 ½ × 8 ½ INCHES

181 (above left)

RATHER THAN A NIGHT OF SILENCE I WOULD EVEN
WELCOME A FEW ILL-CONSIDERED REMARKS
Signed and inscribed with title
Ink and watercolour
9 ½ x 7 ½ INCHES

182 (above)

I DISAPPROVE OF WHAT YOU SAY, BUT I WILL DEFEND TO
THE DEATH YOUR RIGHT TO SAY IT
Signed
Ink and watercolour
9 ¼ x 7 INCHES
Illustrated: *Punch*, 1996

183 (left)

WHILE YOU WERE OUT BOB KERRY PHONED ABOUT THE
BENSON PROJECT. BERT ROSS CALLED TO CONFIRM
LUNCH, AND YOUR WIFE PHONED TO SAY SHE HADN'T
FORGIVEN YOU FOR YOUR BREAKFAST TANTRUMS
Inscribed with title
Ink and watercolour with bodycolour; 10 x 8 INCHES

184 *(above)*

WELL, BESTWICK, WE'VE BOTH BENEFITTED FROM THIS WAGE BARGAINING SESSIONS. I KNOW WHY YOU WANT MORE, AND YOU KNOW WHY I CAN'T GIVE IT
Signed and inscribed with title
Ink and watercolour
10 x 8 INCHES

185 *(above right)*

I REALISE, TEMPKINS, YOU COULDN'T POSSIBLY EXIST ON WHAT YOU'RE WORTH, BUT YOU'RE GETTING CONSIDERABLY MORE THAN THAT ALREADY
Signed and inscribed with title
Ink and watercolour
9 ¾ x 8 ¼ INCHES

186 *(right)*

I'M AFRAID, SIMPSON, YOU'LL HAVE TO GO. WE'RE NOT GEARED UP SUFFICIENTLY FOR YOUR HIGH-POWERED DYNAMIC DRIVE
Signed and inscribed with title
Ink and watercolour with bodycolour
9 ½ x 7 ¼ INCHES

If I were involved in any shenanign I can assure you it would be at top bracket level!

"I've never kidded myself. I've always known I wasn't as good as I thought I was!"

187

IF I WERE INVOLVED IN ANY SHENANIGAN I CAN ASSURE
YOU IT WOULD BE AT TOP BRACKET LEVEL
Signed and inscribed with title
Ink and watercolour
8 ½ × 7 ½ inches
Illustrated: Sunday Telegraph, 6 December 1998, 'Scully's View'

188

I'VE NEVER KIDDED MYSELF. I'VE ALWAYS KNOWN
I WASN'T AS GOOD AS I THOUGHT I WAS
Signed and inscribed with title
Ink and watercolour with bodycolour
10 ¼ × 7 ½ inches

Michael ffolkes

"what do you mean, no?"

MICHAEL FFOLKES

MICHAEL FFOLKES
Michael ffolkes (1925-1988)

An adept watercolourist who worked with a free-flowing, sensual line, Michael ffolkes produced elegant, stylish and flamboyant cartoons, often featuring mythological subjects and adorned with large, sexy ladies.

Michael ffolkes was born Brian Davis in London on 6 June 1925, the son of Walter Lawrence Davis, a commercial artist. He attended Leigh Hall College, a boarding school in Essex, before studying under John Farleigh at St Martin's School of Art from 1941-1943. In 1942, aged 17, he had his first cartoon published in *Punch*. On leaving college, Davis worked in various commercial art studios, before joining the Royal Navy in 1943, where he served as a telegraphist in the Far East. Following the end of the Second World War, he returned to his studies, enrolling at Chelsea School of Art in 1946. It was here that he adopted the name 'Michael ffolkes', chosen at random from Burke's Peerage. It was at this time that his cartoons began appearing regularly in the

Strand Magazine, Lilliput and *Punch*. He also exhibited at the Royal Academy Summer Exhibition whilst still a student. He turned professional soon after graduating in 1949 and in 1953 he published the first collection of his cartoons, titled *ffolkes' ffanfare!* In 1955, he began work with the *Daily Telegraph*, an association that would last for 30 years, illustrating the 'Way of the World' column four days a week, first with Colin Welch and later with Michael Wharton. In 1960, his work was published in *Playboy* for the first time, beginning an association with the magazine that would last for 20 years. He always considered himself a *Punch* cartoonist at heart and in addition to regularly contributing cartoons; he produced a number of *Punch* covers and also began producing caricatures to accompany film reviews from 1961. He considered it one of the greatest honours of his career when he joined the *Punch* table in 1978.

Ffolkes was also a prolific book illustrator, collaborating on over 50 books, including his own works, *ffolkes Fauna* (1977) and *ffolkes' Cartoon Companion to Classical Mythology* (1978). An exhibition of his cinema caricatures was held at the National Film Theatre, London in 1982, and his autobiography was published in 1985 to coincide with further exhibitions at the Palace Theatre and Royal Festival Hall. Ffolkes' work continued to appear in numerous publications throughout his career, such as *Country Fair, Spectator, Private Eye, New Yorker* and *Reader's Digest*. He died in London on 18 October 1988.

189
WHAT DO YOU MEAN, NO?
Signed and inscribed with title
Watercolour and ink
10 ½ x 12 ½ INCHES

191

OH HIM, HE'S THINK NO EVIL
Signed and inscribed with title
Watercolour and ink
8 ¾ × 10 INCHES

190

WELL, WHERE DO YOU THINK IT SHOULD GO?
Signed and inscribed with title
Watercolour and ink
11 ¼ × 9 ¾ INCHES

192

I LOVE YOU, BUT I DON'T THINK WE'RE THE SAME SPECIES
Signed and inscribed with title
Watercolour and ink with bodycolour
10 × 14 ¼ INCHES

193
STRAIGHT OR WITH A LITTLE PIETY?
Signed and inscribed with title
Watercolour and ink
10 ½ x 13 ¼ INCHES

194 *(above right)*
GEORGE, I THINK YOU'VE
WATCHED ONE W C
FIELDS MOVIE TOO MANY
Signed and inscribed with title
Watercolour and ink
10 ½ x 8 ½ INCHES

195 *(left)*
BUSINESS IS TERRIBLE
Signed and inscribed with title
Ink with watercolour
11 x 7 ½ INCHES

196 *(right)*
ALCOHOL BAROMETER
Signed
Watercolour and ink
9 ¼ x 6 ½ INCHES

*"It's a bogus
domestic Burgundy
without any quality but I think
you'll be stupefied
by the price."*

198
A LITTLE MORE OF EXHIBIT B, SERJEANT
Signed and inscribed with title
Watercolour and ink
8 ¾ × 9 ¾ INCHES

197
IT'S A BOGUS DOMESTIC BURGUNDY WITHOUT ANY
QUALITY BUT I THINK YOU'LL BE STUPEFIED BY THE PRICE
Signed with initials and inscribed 'after Th'
Watercolour, ink and collage
13 × 8 ½ INCHES
Illustrated: *Punch*, 26 October 1977, front cover

199
HE ATTEMPTED TO ADD SALT
Signed and inscribed with title
Watercolour and ink
10 × 9 ¼ INCHES

200 *(left)*
THE KIDS SAY I'M ATTRIBUTED TO FRANCIS BACON
Signed
Watercolour, ink and collage
24 × 20 INCHES
Illustrated: *Punch*, 28 March 1979, front cover

201 *(above)*
EXTRAORDINARY, THEY'VE BEEN AROUND FOR CENTURIES
Signed and inscribed with title
Watercolour and ink
11 × 11 ½ INCHES

202 *(left)*
I WOULDN'T SAY THAT YOU DON'T SATISFY ME,
GEORGE. IT'S JUST THAT, ON THE WHOLE, I WOULD
PREFER A LARGE RAVIOLI
Signed, inscribed 'ffor George' and dated '25 II 81'
Watercolour, ink and collage
9 ½ × 13 ½ INCHES

John Glashan

JOHN GLASHAN

JOHN GLASHAN

John Glashan (1927-1999)

John Glashan was best known as the creator of the cartoon strip, 'Genius', which developed a cult following during its five-year run in the *Observer*. His passion for fine watercolour painting allowed him to develop his world of tiny figures inhabiting beautiful, vast, baroque interiors and sweeping landscapes.

For a biography of John Glashan, please refer to *The Illustrators*, 2017, page 216.

Nos **203-217** are all Provenance: the Artist's Estate

203

DINING TABLE FOR SOMEONE WHO WANTS TO BE THE CENTRE OF ATTENTION
Signed
Watercolour with ink and bodycolour
11 x 14 INCHES
Illustrated: *Spectator*, 28 September 1991

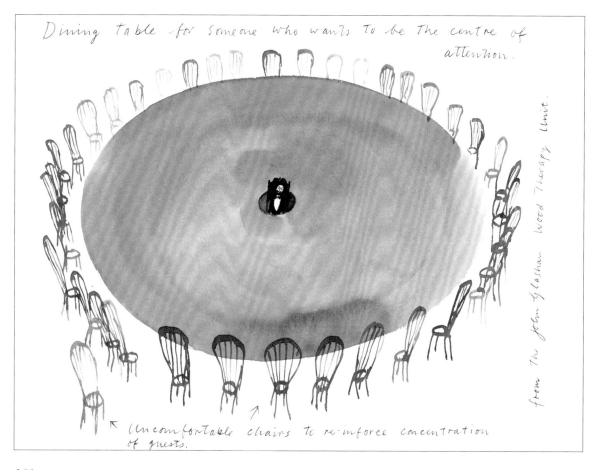

204

A RECENT OPINION POLL REVEALS THAT NINE OUT OF TEN PEOPLE WOULD BE CONTENT TO LIVE UNDER A PERPETUAL SHOWER OF CARBON GRANULES, POWDERED GLASS, WHITE-HOT IRON SHARDS AND NON-SPECIFIC BACTERIA, PROVIDED THAT TWO PERCENT OF THE WORLD'S POPULATION HAD ACCESS TO A CONSTANT SUPPLY OF ANTIQUE SILVERWARE

Signed
Watercolour with ink and bodycolour
16 ½ x 21 ¼ INCHES
Illustrated: *Spectator*, 9 February 1991
Literature: *John Glashan's World*, London: Robinson Publishing, 1991, page 42

A recent opinion poll reveals that nine out of ten people would be content to live under a perpetual shower of carbon granules, powdered glass, white-hot iron shards and non-specific bacteria, provided that two per cent of the world's population had access to a constant supply of antique silverware.

Man does not live by bread alone.

Of course he doesn't, he needs fast cars, yachts, jewellery, pouting women, champagne, skiing, executive jets. Châteaux, Chinese Neolithic pottery... black leather wall coverings...

205
MAN DOES NOT LIVE BY BREAD ALONE
Signed
Watercolour with ink and bodycolour
10 ½ × 14 ¾ INCHES
Illustrated: *Spectator*, 30 July 1994

Sometimes I feel that I won't be able to carry on with my work.

What is your work?

Staring blankly into space with a faraway look in my eyes.

206
SOMETIMES I FEEL THAT I WON'T BE ABLE TO CARRY ON
WITH MY WORK
Signed
Watercolour with ink and bodycolour
14 ½ × 21 INCHES
Illustrated: *Spectator*, 25 June 1994

'WHO ARE YOU?'
'I AM GOD. AND YOU?'
'I AM A MASTER OF RELIGION.'
'RELIGION? WHAT'S THAT?'
Signed
Watercolour with ink and bodycolour
15 × 22 INCHES
Illustrated: *Spectator*, 6 June 1992

208
'FEELING LESS GUILTY, NOW?'
'YES, THANK YOU.'
Signed
Watercolour with ink
11 × 14 INCHES
Illustrated: *Spectator*, 20 March 1993

The Waves of Pain
Course Through the Brain
Legacy of Grape and Grain
Unsheathed Nerve Ends
Hypodermic Rain
Swills Will to Live
Down Insane
Drain

Same again?

Vodka Plain with Novocain

209
THE WAVES OF PAIN COURSE
THROUGH THE BRAIN
LEGACY OF GRAPE AND GRAIN
UNSHEATHED NERVE ENDS
HYPODERMIC RAIN
SWILLS WILL TO LOVE
DOWN INSANE
DRAIN

Signed
Watercolour with ink and bodycolour
10 ¾ × 14 ¼ INCHES
Illustrated: *Spectator*, 31 December 1994

210
'YOU'VE HAD A HEAD JOB? IT SUITS YOU.'
'YES, I FEEL VERY RELAXED AND COMFORTABLE. THEY'VE
MADE ME CHAIRMAN OF THE BANK AND THEY'VE ASKED ME
TO STAND FOR PARLIAMENT. ON SATURDAY, I WON A PRIZE
FOR BALLROOM DANCING ...'
Signed
Watercolour with ink
10 ¾ × 15 INCHES
Illustrated: *Spectator*, 19 March 1994

211

IF YOU HAD THE CHOICE OF ONLY ONE WORD TO USE FOR
THE REST OF YOUR LIFE, WHICH ONE WOULD YOU PICK?
Signed
Watercolour with ink and bodycolour
14 ½ × 22 INCHES
Illustrated: *Spectator*, 18 September 1993

Heh, heh, heh.

212
HEH, HEH, HEH
Signed
Watercolour with ink and bodycolour
10 ¼ × 14 INCHES
Illustrated: *Spectator*, 23 July 1994

213
THE FAVOURITE FOR THIS YEARS' TURNER PRIZE
IS, 'TABLE LYING ON ITS SIDE WITH WRITING
ON IT' BY SEBASTIAN VELCRO
Signed
Watercolour with ink and bodycolour
14 ¾ × 22 INCHES
Illustrated: *Spectator*, 12 November 1994

Come and meet my new dog –
he's a cross between a pirhana
and a cheetah.

214
COME AND MEET MY NEW DOG – HE'S A CROSS
BETWEEN A PIRANHA AND A CHEETAH
Signed
Watercolour with ink and bodycolour
11 x 14 ½ INCHES
Illustrated: *Spectator*, 1 June 1991

The most exciting heavyweight contest of all time, will take place on Saturday night between Winston (RETINA DETACHER) Kierkegaard and

Leroy (BRAIN WASTER) Beegrave —

At the weigh-in.

Well, Detacher, how do you think you'll fare against Belgrave?

Ah'll waste his brain.

215
THE MOST EXCITING HEAVYWEIGHT CONTEST OF ALL TIME,
WILL TAKE PLACE ON SATURDAY NIGHT BETWEEN WINSTON
(RETINA DETACHER) KIERKEGAARD AND LEROY
(BRAIN WASTER) BEEGRAVE
Signed
Watercolour with ink and bodycolour
11 x 15 INCHES
Illustrated: *Spectator*, 7 November 1992

216
A WATCHED KETTLE BE NEVER BOILING
Signed
Watercolour with ink
10 ¾ x 15 INCHES
Illustrated: *Spectator*, 8 June 1991

It's Methylated Mary, nine hundred and fifty eight million, two hundred and seventy-one Thousand, three hundred and forty-sixth in line to the throne...

217
IT'S METHYLATED MARY, NINE HUNDRED AND FIFTY EIGHT
MILLION, TWO HUNDRED AND SEVENTY-ONE THOUSAND,
THREE HUNDRED AND FORTY-SIXTH IN LINE TO THE THRONE ...
Signed
Watercolour with ink
11 ½ × 16 INCHES
Illustrated: *Spectator*, 11 November 1989
Literature: *John Glashan's World*, London: Robinson Publishing, 1991, page 12

Willie Rushton

WILLIE *12* RUSHTON

WILLIE RUSHTON
William George Rushton (1937-1996)

Prolific and highly successful not only as cartoonist and illustrator, but also as writer, actor and comedian, Willie Rushton began his career at the forefront of the 1960s satire boom as a co-founder of the magazine *Private Eye*. He achieved lasting fame on the BBC television series *That Was the Week That Was*, alongside the likes of David Frost, before garnering a cult following on the BBC Radio 4 game show, *I'm Sorry I Haven't a Clue*, from 1974 until his death. He was the author and illustrator of a number of bestselling books, such as *How to Play Football: The Art of Dirty Play* and *Pigsticking: A Joy for Life*.

Willie Rushton was born in Chelsea, London, on 18 August 1937, the only child of John Atherton Rushton, a publisher, and his wife Veronica (neé James). He attended Shrewsbury School from 1950, where he met his future *Private Eye* colleagues Richard Ingrams and Christopher Booker. He showed an early talent for cartooning by producing illustrations for *The Wallopian*, a satirical version of the school magazine *The Salopian*, which he produced with Ingrams and Booker. He struggled academically however, claiming to have failed his mathematics O-level seven times. His failure to achieve a Latin O-Level cost him the chance to join his friends at Oxford, and instead he served his two years of national service. He returned to civilian life as a solicitor's clerk in 1959. During this time he regularly sent cartoons to *Punch*, none of which were accepted. After quitting his job as a clerk, he worked at the *Liberal News*, producing the weekly strip, 'Brimstone Belchers', between June 1960 and March 1961, and a weekly political cartoon until 1962. He had remained in contact with his friends at Oxford, where Ingrams was editing two magazines, *Mesopotamia* and *Parson's Pleasure*, to which he contributed cartoons. Between them they conceived the idea for a London-based satirical magazine whilst in a Chelsea pub, and the first issue of *Private Eye* was published on 25 October 1961, with Rushton producing all the illustrations. Early issues of the paper were put together in Rushton's bedroom in his mother's house in Kensington.

Having developed a taste for acting whilst accompanying his friends from Shrewsbury in a well-received revue at the Edinburgh Fringe, Willie Rushton made his professional stage debut in 1961 in Spike Milligan's *The Bed-Sitting Room*, at the Marlowe Theatre in Canterbury. Not long after, he appeared in cabaret with Richard Ingrams, John Wells and Barbara Windsor at the Room at the Top, a nightclub above a department store in Ilford, east London. Here, Rushton's impersonation of Prime Minister Harold Macmillan caught the attention of a BBC producer and, from November 1962 to December 1963, he appeared in the BBC programme *That Was the Week That Was*, which drew in audiences of up to 13 million and found him immediate fame. In 1965, he met Arlene Dorgan while hosting the variety entertainment show *New Stars and Garters*. They married in 1968 and together had one son. Though *That Was the Week That Was* was cancelled in 1964, he continued to work regularly on television, appearing in *Not Only… But Also* with Peter Cook and Dudley Moore and episodes of popular series such as *Up Pompeii!* (1970), *The Persuaders!* (1971) and *Colditz* (1974). On stage, he appeared in *Gulliver's Travels* at the Mermaid in 1971 and 1979, and in Eric Idle's *Pass the Butler* at the Globe in 1982. He also had a series of cameo roles in films such as *Magnificent Men in their Flying Machines* (1965) and *Monte Carlo or Bust* (1969). Between 1985 and 1989, Willie Rushton was a regular panellist on the television show *Celebrity Squares* and a popular story reader on the children's show *Jackanory*.

Willie Rushton achieved perhaps his widest following and greatest popularity on BBC Radio 4's *I'm Sorry I Haven't a Clue*, which he joined in 1974 and appeared as a regular team member in every yearly series until his death. He appeared alongside fellow comedians such as Tim Brooke Taylor, Graeme Garden and Barry Cryer. In 1996, he teamed up with Barry Cryer, in their own show, *Two Old Farts in the Night*, performing to full audiences at the Edinburgh Festival, Royal Albert Hall and Royal Festival Hall.

Having not been involved in *Private Eye* since the later years of the 1960s, Willie Rushton returned in 1978 to illustrate 'Mrs Wilson's Diary' and 'Auberon Waugh's Diary'. When Waugh moved to the *Daily Telegraph* in the mid-1980s, Rushton followed, while also contributing to his *Literary Review*, providing the monthly coloured covers, while at the same time producing fortnightly caricatures for *Private Eye*'s literary review page. He contributed a regular contents-page illustration to the *Independent Magazine*, and from 1993 to 1996 drew cartoons for Channel 4's television series *Rory Bremner… Who Else?*. He also published a number of his own humorous books, including *How to Play Football: The Art of Dirty Play* (1968), *Pigsticking, a Joy for Life: a Gentleman's Guide to Sporting Pastimes* (1977), *Bureaucrats: how to Annoy*

Them (under the pseudonym R. T. Fishall) (1981), and *Willie Rushton's Great Moments in History* (1984). The original artwork for this latter work was commissioned as a permanent collection at the Victoria and Albert Museum.

Willie Rushton was a passionate cricket fan throughout his life. He received coaching at Lord's as a boy, later playing for the Lord's Taverners, and was a regular team captain on BBC Radio 4's quiz show, *Trivia Test Match*, running from 1986 to 1993. His 1984 novel, *W. G. Grace's Last Case*, was based on a fictional episode in the life of the great cricketer.

He died from complications after heart surgery at Cromwell Hospital, Kensington on 11 December 1996, aged 59.

No **232**, please see page 192

218
MARTIN AMIS AS ROBOCOP
Signed with initial and dated 91
Ink
8 × 7 ½ INCHES
Illustrated: *Literary Review*, September 1991, cover,
Adam Mars-Jones (reviewer), 'Times Arrow' by Martin Amis

219
IT'S YOUR BIRD-BATH, UNGRATEFUL FOWL
Ink and watercolour
9 ½ × 7 ¼ INCHES
Illustrated: Frank Ward and William Rushton, *Unarmed Gardening.*
How To Tame The Thing Outside, London: Macdonald and Jane's, 1977,
page 117, 'Finding Something To Do'

220
ANTI-THRIPP
Ink
9 ½ × 7 ½ INCHES
Illustrated: Frank Ward and William Rushton, *Unarmed Gardening.*
How To Tame The Thing Outside, London: Macdonald and Jane's, 1977,
page 100, 'Squirting'

221
A TALE OF
HORTICULTURAL
ESPIONAGE
Ink
9 ½ × 7 ¼ INCHES
Illustrated: Frank Ward and William
Rushton, *Unarmed Gardening. How
To Tame The Thing Outside*, London:
Macdonald and Jane's, 1977, page
40, 'Escape Routes Survivors'

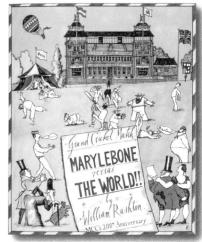

'I refer, Mr Chairman, to the lavatory at the Nursery End – the Gentlemen's lavatory, I hasten to add – with the corollary that the term "Gentlemen" is used advisedly as a close inspection of the building will reveat that it is no more than a Post Restante for every homosexualist — every pervert –'

'Are you suggesting, Sir, that homosexuals pursue the Noble Game?'

(*Marylebone Versus the World*, page 41)

222
MINUTES OF THE MCC BUILDINGS AND WORKS COMMITTEE
Ink
10 x 7 ½ inches
Illustrated: William Rushton, *Marylebone Versus the World*, London: Pavilion, 1987, page 40

223
SNOOKER
POTTING AND PUTTING
Ink
9 ¼ × 7 INCHES
Illustrated: William Rushton,
Pigsticking. A Joy For Life, A
 Gentleman's Guide to Sporting
Pastimes, London: Macdonald and
Jane's, 1977, 'Snooker', page 116

224
FREDDIE TRUEMAN AND
ERIC MORECAMBE
Ink
8 ½ × 5 INCHES
Illustrated: Fred Trueman,
The Thoughts of Trueman Now,
London: Macdonald and Jane's,
1978, page 9

3.8.79
THE BEST THINGS on television this summer at the National Health Council advertisements warning parents not to overfeed their disgusting, football-like, toothless children.

...Was it the world's worst party, guests asked themselves as they were ushered out of *Punch* magazine's relaunch celebration at Harrods on the dot of nine o'clock on Tuesday night?
   The heat was intense, the drink in short supply, there were far too many people and too many of them were ugly, and unknown to anyone but themselves. But humorists are often ugly and nearly always unknown...
7th September 1996

225
PUNCH'S RELAUNCH
PARTY
Signed with initial
Text signed by Auberon Waugh
Ink
4 ¼ × 2 ¾ INCHES
Illustrated: *Daily Telegraph*,
7 September 1996, 'Way of the World' by Auberon Waugh

226
THE BEST THINGS ON
TELEVISION
Text signed by Auberon Waugh
Ink; 5 ¾ × 5 ¼ INCHES
Illustrated: Auberon Waugh, *The Diaries of Auberon Waugh*, London:
Private Eye, 3 August 1979
Exhibited: 'Private Eye Cartoonists: the 50th Anniversary', Chris Beetles Gallery, London, October-November 2011, no 125

227

TO BRIGHTON WITH A HUGE
PARTY OF LORD GNOME'S
MINIONS WHERE WE
CELEBRATE P.G. WODEHOUSE'S
CENTENARY WITH A FEAST
IN THE ROYAL PAVILION
Signed with initial and dated 81
Text signed by Auberon Waugh
Pen and ink
4 ½ × 7 INCHES
Illustrated: *Private Eye*, 23 October 1981;
Auberon Waugh, *The Diaries of Auberon
Waugh*, London: Private Eye/Andre
Deutsch, 1985, page 133
Exhibited: '40 Years of Private Eye',
Chris Beetles Gallery, London, October-
November 2001, No 124;
'Private Eye Cartoonists: the 50th
Anniversary', Chris Beetles Gallery,
London, October-November 2011

23.10.81
TO BRIGHTON with a huge party of Lord Gnome's minions where we celebrate
P.G. Wodehouse's centenary with a feast in the Royal Pavilion.

228

THE AUSTRALIANS
Signed with initial and dated '92
Ink
7 × 10 ½ INCHES
Illustrated: *Sunday Telegraph*

Harold had a go at joining the Common Market. 'I cannot see', he said over a cup of tea, 'how General de Gaulle can say "No".' General de Gaulle said 'NON!!'. 'I hadn't thought of that,' said Harold, helping himself to a spoonful of Delikat. Then he devalued the Pound. 'This', he said, 'does not mean the Pound in your pocket has been devalued.' You couldn't help liking the old rogue. Well, some didn't and he lost an election to Edward Heath. But four years later he was back. This time by three votes and still puffing away on his pipe. In public that was. The moment he was back in Number Ten, it was out with the jukebox and Party Tim!

You'd never have guessed from all this just how grim things were, with talk of Military Coups, the International Monetary Fund cancelling our overdraft, and the KGB under the kitchen table at Number Ten. It was all very confusing, certainly for a cat.

(Humphrey, *The Nine Lives of the Number Ten Cat*, page 22)

229
'LET'S BOOGY!' CRIED HAROLD, 'LET'S BOP TO THE BEAT. AND CAT, THROW THOSE SEVEN MICE INTO THE STREET'
Ink
10 ½ × 8 INCHES
Provenance: Dr Aidan Mcgennis
Illustrated: Willie Rushton, *Humphrey, The Nine Lives of the Number Ten Cat*, London: Pavilion Books, 1995, page 23

The dustmen stopped working. All the gravediggers stopped working. I refused to leave the premises. It was very unpleasant out. Chaos. Certainly Unfit for Cats.

In a way, you had to admire old Jim. In the middle of all this, like Lord Nelson before him, Jim said, 'I see no chaos'. Admittedly, when he said it he was on his way back from a Summit Conference in sunny Guadeloupe. He then lost a vote of 'no confidence' in the House of Commons by one vote, the one vote being a mad Scots Nat, thus ushering in One Hundred Years of Mrs Thatcher.

(Humphrey, *The Nine Lives of the Number Ten Cat*, page 26)

230

'THEY'RE ALL ON STRIKE' SAID HONEST JIM, 'EXCEPT TEN BLASTED MICE. GET RID OF THEM, CAT!'
'I'M GOING SLOW' I SAID 'BUT NAME YOUR PRICE'

Ink

9 ½ × 8 INCHES

Provenance: Dr Aidan Mcgennis
Illustrated: Willie Rushton, *Humphrey, The Nine Lives of the Number Ten Cat*, London: Pavilion Books, 1995, page 27

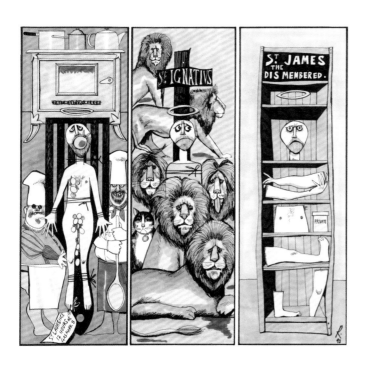

231
SAINTLY LIVES AND
GRUESOME DEATHS
Signed with initial and dated 1993
Ink
10 × 10 ½ INCHES
Illustrated: *Literary Review*, August
1993, cover, Brian Masters
(reviewer), Jacobus De Voragine,
The Golden Legend, Princeton:
Princeton University Press, 1993

232 *(left)*
THE END
Ink
3 ¼ × 3 INCHES
Illustrated: Jon Talbot, *Elephant on
the Line!*, London: Kaye and Ward,
1979
Exhibited: 'Quick on the Draw,
Drawings by Willie Rushton',
Shrewsbury Museum & Art
Gallery, April 2004, No 20

233
JOAN SMITH,
ADAM AND EVE
Signed with initial
Ink
11 × 10 ¾ INCHES
Illustrated: *Literary Review*,
November 1996, cover, Lisa
Jardine (reviewer) of Joan Smith,
*Hungry For You: From Cannibalism
To Seduction*, London: Chatto and
Windus, 1996

The Americans

THE AMERICANS

WILLIAM STEIG
William Steig (1907-2003)

The American artist, William Steig, first made his name with his highly original cartoons for *The New Yorker*, and he worked regularly for that magazine for several decades. Gradually, he widened his reputation with his work as a draughtsman and sculptor. Then from his sixties, he gained an entirely new audience – and many prizes – as an illustrator and writer of popular children's books, including *Shrek!* (1990), which proved the basis for the phenomenally popular series of animated films.

For a biography of William Steig, please refer to *The Illustrators*, 2020, page 180.

Further reading:
Claudia J Nahson, *The Art of William Steig*, Yale University Press, 2007

234
MEET THE WIFE
Signed
Inscribed with title below mount
Ink
5 ½ x 4 ½ INCHES

235
ANNABELLE MAKES A BEAUTIFUL HOME
Signed
Inscribed with title below mount
Ink
5 ½ x 4 ½ INCHES

Nos **234-237** are all illustrated in William Steig, *Till Death Do Us Part: some ballet notes on marriage*, New York: Duell, Sloan and Pearce, 1947

236
WHEN YOU AND I WERE YOUNG, MAGGIE
Signed
Inscribed with title below mount
Ink
5 ½ × 4 ½ INCHES

237
I ALWAYS PUT MY FOOT IN IT
Signed
Inscribed with title below mount
Ink
5 ¼ × 4 ½ INCHES

BUD HANDELSMAN
John Bernard Handelsman (1922-2007)

J B Handelsman achieved great popularity on both sides of the Atlantic as a cartoonist for *The New Yorker*, *Punch* and *Playboy*. Though perhaps best known in the UK as the creator of the strip, 'Freaky Fables', which ran for 11 years in *Punch*, his meticulous line and particularly the sharp, dry wit of his captions stood him out as one of the finest and most memorable *New Yorker* cartoonists of the twentieth century.

J B Handelsman was born Bernard Handelsman in Manhattan, New York, on 5 February 1922. His father, Max Handelsman, was born in New York of Jewish Hungarian immigrants and taught English at the James Monroe High School in the Bronx. His mother, Dinah (née Birnbaum) was also a teacher. His sister, Edith, was eight years his senior and would become a journalist and writer working under the nom de plume Edith Anderson.

He began drawing cartoons as a young boy, and had decided upon a career as a comic strip artist by the age of ten.

As a child, Handelsman grew up in the Bronx and was educated in the Bronx public school system, before studying at the Art Students' League from 1938 to 1942. After the USA entered the Second World War, he enlisted briefly in the US Army Air Corps, though he was discharged in 1945 due to his suffering from asthma. Later that year, he enrolled at New York University to study electrical engineering. However, in 1946, he left university in order to pursue a career as a commercial artist, and began working as a typographic designer in various New York advertising agencies. At this time, he also began working as a freelance cartoonist, submitting cartoons to magazines and newspapers such as *Playboy*, *Esquire* and *The Saturday Evening Post*. As a cartoonist, he began to use the professional name 'J B Handelsman'. He had always disliked the name given to him at birth, and as an adult had adopted the name John, though he was known informally as 'Bud'. In 1960, he began freelance cartooning full-time and the following year submitted his first cartoon to *The New Yorker,* beginning an association with the magazine that would continue for 45 years.

In 1963, he moved to England with his wife, Gertrude (née Peck), whom he had married in 1950, and his three children, and settled in Leatherhead, Surrey. He believed that his style of cartooning and sense of humour were more suited to a British audience, and he began contributing regular cartoons to *Punch*, as well as to the *Evening Standard*, *Observer*, *New Statesman* and *Saturday Review*. He found particular popularity with his weekly cartoon series, 'Freaky Fables', which ran in *Punch* for 11 years. Handelsman was also a talented writer and regularly submitted short stories to *Punch* under an assortment of pseudonyms. His cartoons to *Punch* were also often submitted under a different pseudonym, such as 'T R Squink' or 'A J Spoop', but his unmistakable line meant that his editors were never in doubt as to who the true creator was.

Handelsman maintained a connection to his native country and continued to submit cartoons to *The New Yorker*, who offered him a contract in 1967, and to *Playboy*. In 1971, *Playboy* published a collection of his cartoons, *You're Not Serious, I Hope*, and in 1978 awarded him their award for Best Black and White Cartoon. He returned to the United States in 1982 and continued to distribute his cartoons widely. He was also sought after as an illustrator of books for adults and for children. He collaborated with John Cleese and the psychiatrist Robin Skinner on *Families and How to Survive Them* (1983) and *Life and How to Survive It* (1993) and with David Frost on *The Mid-Atlantic Companion* (1986). John Cleese referred to Handelsman as 'the best cartoonist alive'. The children's books he illustrated included *Who's That Stepping on Plymouth Rock?* (1975) by Jean Fritz and *The Funny Side of Science* (1973) by Melvin Berger. In 1992, he created a 10-minute animated film called 'In the Beginning' based on the Creation, which was broadcast on BBC television on Christmas Eve of that year.

Handelsman continued to appear weekly in *The New Yorker* until 2006. Over the course of his career he contributed just under 1,000 cartoons for the magazine, along with five covers. He died of lung cancer at his home in Southampton, New York, on 20 June 2007.

Further Reading:

Mark Jacobs, *Jumping Up and Down on the Roof, Throwing Bags of Water on People*, *Garden City*, NY: Doubleday, 1980

238
IF I HAVE TO ASK PERMISSION FOR EVERY BITE, DEAREST, WE'LL BE MATING ALL DAY
Signed
Ink and watercolour
6 ¼ x 4 ½ INCHES
Illustrated: *The New Yorker*, 18 October 1993, page 81

239
THE SAINTLY BEATLES
Signed
Ink and watercolour with gold pen and collage
12 ½ × 10 ¼ INCHES
Illustrated: *Punch*, 23 November 1966, front cover

240 *(above)*
THAT WAS A FINE REPORT, BARBARA. BUT SINCE THE
SEXES SPEAK DIFFERENT LANGUAGES, I PROBABLY DIDN'T
UNDERSTAND A WORD OF IT
Signed
Ink and watercolour
4 ¾ × 6 INCHES
Illustrated: *The New Yorker*, 30 January 1995, page 77

241 *(above right)*
NEVER MIND WHAT I <u>DID</u>, YOUR HONOR. I WANT
TO BE JUDGED FOR WHO I AM, AS AN INDIVIDUAL
Signed
Ink and watercolour
6 ½ × 5 ½ INCHES
Illustrated: *The New Yorker*, 24 February 1997, page 102

242 *(left)*
IN MY YOUNGER DAYS, I HAD NEVER HEARD OF SUCH
THINGS AS RADICCHIO OR ARUGULA, AND NOW THAT
I'VE HEARD OF THEM IT HASN'T BROUGHT ME HAPPINESS
Signed and inscribed with title
Ink and watercolour
7 ½ × 8 ¾ INCHES
Illustrated: *Playboy*

243
'IN FLAGRANTE DELICTO', INDEED! YOU NEVER MISS
AN OPPORTUNITY TO SHOW OFF YOUR CLASSICAL
EDUCATION, DO YOU?
Signed
Ink and watercolour
7 x 5 ½ INCHES
Illustrated: *The New Yorker*, 17 January 2000, page 62

244
THERE IT IS! YOU SEE? RIGHT THERE IN THE TALMUD!
'FEED A COLD AND STARVE A FEVER'
Signed and inscribed with title
Ink and watercolour with bodycolour
7 x 8 ¾ INCHES
Illustrated: *Playboy*

245

WHAT A GLORIOUS SUNSET, EH? AND YOU COMPLAIN
ABOUT THE KIND OF WORLD I'VE GIVEN YOU
Signed and inscribed with title
Ink and watercolour with bodycolour
12 × 7 ¾ INCHES
Illustrated: *Playboy*, May 1970, page 189

246

THEN I SAID, 'NO, DAMN IT! I'VE STILL GOT SOME
INTEGRITY!' AND I REFUSED TO PUT IN ANY
MORE MEAT BALLS
Signed and inscribed with title
Ink watercolour and bodycolour
13 ½ × 9 ½ INCHES
Illustrated: *Playboy*

DAVID LEVINE
David Levine (1926-2009)

David Levine was widely acknowledged as one of the greatest, and most influential, caricaturists of the second half of the 20th century. Best known as the staff artist of *The New York Review of Books*, he revived the tradition of American political caricature that originated in the nineteenth century with Thomas Nast, and has been frequently described as equal to Honoré Daumier. However, he sustained an equally distinguished career as a painter, producing figurative oils and watercolours in a poetically naturalistic style. His love of Corot and Vuillard, Eakins and Sargent, pervades his studies of Coney Island and the Garment District. But more fundamental to both his paintings and his caricatures is the fact that he said, 'I love my species'.

For a biography of David Levine, please refer to *The Illustrators*, 2010, pages 277-278

247 (below left)
EZRA POUND AND T S ELIOT
Signed and dated 71
Inscribed 'T S Eliot' on reverse
Ink; 12 ½ × 8 ½ INCHES
Illustrated: *The New York Review of Books*, 18 November 1971, 'The First Waste Land' by Richard Ellmann (A Review of the Waste Land Annotations of Ezra Pound)

248 (below right)
SAMUEL PEPYS
Signed and dated 70
Inscribed 'Pepys' and 'N Y Review of Books' and dated 1970 on reverse
Ink; 13 × 11 INCHES
Illustrated: *The New York Review of Books*, 8 October 1970, 'O Calcutta! by Matthew Hodgart, a review of the *Diary of Samuel Pepys*, edited by Robert Latham and William Matthews

249
SALMAN RUSHDIE
Signed and dated 96; Inscribed 'S Rushdie' on reverse
Ink
13 ¾ × 10 INCHES
Illustrated: *The New York Review of Books*, 21 March 1996, 'Palimpsest Regained'
by J M Coetzee (a Review of Salman Rushdie's The Moor's Last Sigh);
The New York Review of Books, 4 October 2001, 'Puppet Show' by
John Leonard (a Review of Salman Rushdie's Fury);
The New York Review of Books, 6 October 2005, 'Massacre in Arcadia'
by Pankaj Mishra (a Review of Salman Rushdie's Shalimar the Clown);
The New York Review of Books, 12 June 2008, 'In The Emperor's Dream House'
by Joyce Carol Oates, a review of the *Enchantress of Florence* by
Salman Rushdie

250
HAROLD PINTER
Signed and dated 70
Inscribed with title on reverse
Ink
9 ½ × 8 INCHES
Illustrated: *The New York Review of Books*, 4 October 2001, 'Harold Pinter's
Celebration' by Daniel Mendelsohn (a review of the productions included in
the Harold Pinter Festival at the Lincoln Centre)

251
COCO CHANEL
Signed and dated 72
Inscribed 'Chanel' on reverse
Ink
12 ½ × 10 INCHES
Illustrated: *The New York Review of Books*, 10 August 1972, 'Living It Out'
by Jean Stafford (a review of three books about Parisian women)

252
W B YEATS
Signed and dated 66
Inscribed 'Yeats' and 'NYR' and dated 1966 on reverse
Ink
12 ½ × 8 INCHES
Illustrated: *The London Review of the Books*, 6 April 1967,
'The Politics of Poetry' by Denis Donoghue

ED SOREL
Edward Sorel (born 1929)

Edward Sorel's clever and unforgiving satire is the product of a lifetime spent observing and criticising the unpleasant reality of the American Dream. His experiences of recent history from the Great Depression to Al-Qaeda, and his disdain for the greasy politics in between, have lent his cartoons a formidable bite that those his junior rarely match.

For a biography of Ed Sorel, please refer to *The Illustrators*, 2020, page 202.

253
AND THE OSCAR DOESN'T GO TO ...
Signed
Ink and watercolour
16 × 24 INCHES
Illustrated: *Vanity Fair*, March 2005

254
RUPERT MURDOCH AS THE
BLOOD-SUCKING FIEND DRACULA
Signed
Pencil sketch of Rupert Murdoch on reverse
Pastel and pencil
24 ½ × 17 ½ INCHES
Illustrated: *Columbia Journalism Review*,
May-June 1984, 'Murdoch Stalks Chicago'
Literature: Ed Sorel, *Unauthorized Portraits*,
New York: Afred A Knopf, 1997, page 127

255
ESTHER BEFORE ASSUERUS
Signed and inscribed with title
Ink and watercolour
13 ½ × 10 ¼ INCHES
Illustrated: Drawn for *The Festival of Purim*, The Jewish Museum,
New York, 2008

256
QUEEN VICTORIA AND ALEXANDER GRAHAM BELL
Signed
Ink and watercolour
16 × 11 ½ INCHES
Illustrated: *New York Observer*

ARNOLD ROTH
Arnold Roth (born 1929)

'Arnold Roth is surely the most imaginative and humorous graphic of this day or any other day. Even Max Beerbohm at his best would have to take a back seat.' (George Plimpton, *Paris Review*)

For a biography of Arnold Roth, please refer to *The Illustrators*, 2015, page 158.

257
DETERGENT QUEEN
Signed
Inscribed with title below mount
Watercolour and bodycolour
12 ½ × 18 INCHES
Illustrated: *TV Guide*, New York

258
GAMESMANSHIP
Signed
Inscribed with title below mount
Watercolour with ink
13 ½ × 8 ½ INCHES
Illustrated: *TV Guide*, New York

259
THE CENSOR
Signed
Inscribed with title of article below mount
Ink and watercolour
13 × 16 INCHES
Illustrated: *TV Guide*, 8 January 1972, page 6, 'From No-No! To Yes, Wow!' by Maurice Zolotow

'The current television season may not be the most innovative in history, but it is surely one of the most uninhibited. and the fact that we are not more shocked by this is a measure of how far we have come, and how fast, in accepting a television freed of the taboos of yesteryear.'
(Maurice Zolotow, page 7)

260
PAMPERED PROFESSIONAL
GOLFER
Signed
Watercolour
5 x 8 ¼ INCHES
Illustrated: *TV Guide*, New York
Exhibited: 'Hole in One!',
The Atkinson Gallery Southport,
May-August 2017

261
ROLLER DERBY
Signed with initials
Inscribed with title below mount
Ink and watercolour with pencil
6 ½ x 17 ½ INCHES
Illustrated: *TV Guide*, New York

262
NHL (NATIONAL HOCKEY LEAGUE) COPS
Signed and inscribed with title
Ink and watercolour
15 ½ × 16 ½ INCHES
Illustrated: *TV Guide*, New York

263
BUT, AS FOR YOU, CHARLIE POMERANTZ ...
Signed
Inscribed with title below mount
Ink and watercolour
10 ½ × 9 ¼ INCHES
Illustrated: *TV Guide*, New York, 30 May 1970

EDWARD KOREN
Edward Koren (born 1935)

Edward Koren is undoubtedly one of the most loved and revered cartoonists in the history of *The New Yorker*. With his first cartoon appearing in 1962, he has since produced over one thousand cartoons, illustrations and covers for the magazine. Famous for his wonderfully fuzzy beasts, Koren delights in making, in his own words, 'the ordinary and mundane hairy and unshorn'.

For a biography of Edward Koren, please refer to *The Illustrators*, 2015, page 170.

264
RUPERT, YOUR LAST RUN WAS
ABSOLUTELY PROFOUND
Signed and inscribed with title
Ink
11 × 13 ¾ INCHES

CONTEMPORARY 14 ILLUSTRATORS

RICHARD SHIRLEY SMITH
Richard Shirley Smith (born 1935)

Self-taught as a wood engraver, Richard Shirley Smith has drawn upon the inspirations of Italian architecture, theatre, poetry and classicism to become recognised as one of Britain's finest classical illustrators and engravers.

Richard Shirley Smith was born in Hampstead in 1935, the son of a Harley Street heart specialist. As a young child, he moved with his family to Brimpton, Berkshire, where he first met the composer, Gerald Finzi and his wife Joy, an artist and writer. The time he spent at their home in Ashmansworth and the rooms there dedicated to reading, composition and sculpture had a profound effect on the young Shirley Smith and the Finzis would remain a strong influence over him throughout his career. He was educated at The Hall School in Hampstead, and at Harrow, where he was taught art by the illustrator Maurice Percival. Whilst boarding at Harrow, he lived next door to the painter and war poet, David Jones. After completing his national service in the Royal Artillery British Army of the Rhine, he studied at the Slade School of Fine Art from 1956 to 1960 under John Aldridge and Anthony Gross.

In 1960, Richard Shirley Smith travelled to Rome with his wife, Juliet Wood, whom he had married that year, and studied there for six months, before travelling to Anticoli Corrado, beyond Tivoli, where he taught himself wood engraving. While in Anticoli Corrado, they were visited by Joy Finzi, who was working on a group of poems entitled *A Point of Departure*, inspired by her grief at the death of her husband. Shirley Smith used his newly acquired skill as a wood engraver to produce seventeen engravings for the poems, which would eventually be published in 1967 by Golden Head Press. On his return to England, he showed these engravings to Anthony Gross, his teacher from the Slade, who subsequently introduced him to Faber & Faber and Oxford University Press. In 1963, he held his first solo exhibition, at the Mount Gallery in Hampstead.

Having settled back in England, Richard Shirley Smith began lecturing part-time at St Albans and Watford School of Art and working as an extra mural lecturer for London and Bristol Universities. In 1966, aged 27, he became the youngest Head of Art to be appointed at Marlborough College, a position he held until 1971. Between 1969 and 1971, he made three research expeditions to the Villas of the Veneto, the results of which were published in a set of four educational slide strips, *The Story of the Venetian Villas*, in 1973.

In 1970, Richard Shirley Smith was commissioned by John Dreyfus, the typographer and agent for the Limited Editions Club of New York, to produce 42 wood engravings for Stephen Spender's *The Poems of Percy Bysshe Shelley*.

When this edition was published the following year, it established his reputation as one of the country's leading and most sought after engravers. In 1973, he illustrated Lord Chesterfield's *Letters to his Son* for the Folio Society, for whom he also illustrated the Earl of Rochester's *Perfect and Imperfect Enjoyment* (1992) and Ovid's *Metamorphoses* (1995). In 1976, he was commissioned to paint a trompe l'oeil for the Doric Villa in Regent's Park, London. This would be the first of twelve such commissions, including one for the Regalian Project at Kensington Palace Gardens in 1991. Since 2002, he has completed a three storey mural at Sheepdrove in Hungerford, Berkshire, entitled *The Cycle of Life*, and the mural *Laskett Shades* for historian Sir Roy Strong.

At the age of fifty, in 1985, Richard Shirley Smith was celebrated with a Retrospective Exhibition that went on display at the Ashmoleon Museum in Oxford and the RIBA Heinz Gallery in London, after which the Ashmoleon acquired a complete set of his wood engravings. In 1994, the collection *The Wood Engravings of Richard Shirley Smith*, written by Iain Bain, was published by Silent Books. His collected bookplates were published by The Fleece Press in 2005.

In May 1999, Chris Beetles Gallery held a major solo exhibition of the work of Richard Shirley Smith.

His work is represented in numerous public collections, including the British Museum and the V&A; the Ashmolean Museum and Bodleian Library (Oxford) and Yale University (New Haven, CT).

> Nos *265-273* are all woodcuts and are illustrated in Stephen Spender (ed), *The Poems of Percy Bysshe Shelley*, Cambridge: Limited Editions Club, 1971

265
'TIS NOTHING
BUT A LITTLE
DOWNY OWL
Signed and dated '71
Inscribed 'Shelley 15'
below mount
3 × 2 ¼ INCHES
Illustrated: page 149

266 (above)
HOMER'S HYMN TO THE SUN
Signed and dated '71
Inscribed 'Shelley 15' below mount
3 ¾ × 2 ¾ INCHES
Illustrated: page 305

267 (above)
THE INVITATION
Signed and dated '71
Inscribed 'Shelley 5' below mount
3 ¾ × 2 ¾ INCHES
Illustrated: page 258

268 (above far right)
EUGANEAN HILLS
Signed and dated '71
Inscribed 'Shelley 6' below mount
4 ¾ × 2 ½ INCHES
Illustrated: page 132

269 (right)
AND ONE KEEN PYRAMID WITH
WEDGE SUBLIME
Signed and dated '71
Inscribed 'Shelley 9' below mount; 2 ×3 ¾ INCHES
Illustrated: page 192

270 *(left)*
THE TWINKLING OF
THINE INFANT HANDS
Signed and dated '71
Inscribed 'Shelley 21' below
mount
2 ½ × 2 ¼ INCHES
Illustrated: page 59

271 *(right)*
THOU HAST LIKE
TO A ROCK –
BUILT REFUGE STOOD
Signed and dated '71
Inscribed 'Shelley 23'
below mount
3 ¾ × 3 INCHES
Illustrated: page 195

272 *(below)*
THE OFFERING
Signed and dated '71
Inscribed 'Shelley 17' below mount
2 × 3 INCHES; Illustrated: title page

273 *(below)*
HELL IS A CITY MUCH LIKE LONDON
Signed and dated '71
Inscribed 'Shelley 38' below mount
1 ¾ × 2 ¼ INCHES; Illustrated: page 208

MICHAEL FOREMAN

Michael Foreman, OBE RDI (born 1938)

While Michael Foreman is perhaps best known as one of the most outstanding contemporary creators of children's books, he is a wide-ranging artist, illustrating literary classics and working as a painter.

For a biography of Michael Foreman, please refer to *The Illustrators*, 2018, pages 132-133

274

PETER PAN

Signed, inscribed with title and dated 1987
Watercolour with pencil, ink and bodycolour
9 ½ × 7 INCHES
Illustrated: J M Barrie, *Peter Pan and Wendy*, London: Pavilion, 1988

In 2017, Chris Beetles Gallery mounted a major retrospective, 'Michael Foreman: Telling Tales', which was accompanied by a fully-illustrated 140-page catalogue.

Recent OBE recipient and award-winning illustrator Michael Foreman has published in the last year:

Please Write Soon: An Unforgettable Story of Two Cousins in World War II, written by Michael Rosen and published by Scholastic in April 2022. *Please Write Soon* is a companion book to *Poppy Field*, written by Michael Morpurgo in 2018, and is inspired by a true family story which explores World War II and the Holocaust.

There Once is a Queen is another collaboration with award winning author Michael Morpurgo, and was published in May 2022 by Harper Collins Children's Books. It is a poetic celebration of Queen Elizabeth's reign, for which the publication coincided with the celebrations for the Platinum Jubilee.

Flying Scotsman and the Best Birthday Ever, written by Michael Morpurgo, marks the centenary year of the famous locomotive the Flying Scotsman. The original illustrations will be exhibited at Danum Gallery, Doncaster, 11 February-17 June 2023 and then journey to Chris Beetles Gallery for an exhibition in July 2023.

NOAH AND THE
LITTLE ELEPHANT

Noah and the Little Elephant was published
in 2021 by Harper Collins Children's
Books in association with the wildlife
conservation charity Tusk. The sensitive
illustrations and heart-warming narrative
of the book draw attention to the
importance of protecting elephants
against poachers.

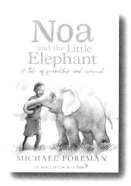

Nos *275-287* are all illustrated in Michael Foreman, *Noa and the
Little Elephant*, London: Harper Collins, 2021, [unpaginated]

275 *(above left)*
NOA AND THE
LITTLE ELEPHANT
Signed, inscribed with title
and dated 2021
Watercolour and pencil
10 ¼ × 7 ¾ INCHES
Illustrated: front cover

276 *(left)*
HE LIKED TO WATCH
ALL THE AMAZING
ANIMALS ATTRACTED
TO THE COOL
WATERS OF THE
GREAT RIVER
Signed and dated 2021
Watercolour and pencil
10 ¾ × 16 ¾ INCHES

277
NOA LOVED BEING ON THE RIVER
Signed and dated 2021
Watercolour and pencil
10 ¼ x 10 INCHES

278
MOST OF ALL, NOA LOVED TO WATCH THE MOTHER
ELEPHANT AND HER BABY
Signed and dated 2021
Watercolour and pencil with bodycolour
10 ½ x 20 INCHES

279 *(opposite above left)*
DAD TOLD NOA ABOUT THE HUNTERS WHO SHOT
ELEPHANTS WITH GUNS AND POISON ARROWS TO
STEAL THEIR VALUABLE TUSKS
Signed and dated 2021
Watercolour and pencil
6 ½ × 6 ½ INCHES

280 *(opposite above right)*
AT FIRST THE BABY ELEPHANT WAS FRIGHTENED
WHEN HE SAW NOA, BUT THEN HE RECOGNISED
HIS RIVERBANK FRIEND
Signed and dated 2021
Watercolour and pencil
8 ¾ × 6 ½ INCHES

282 *(below)*
IN THE NEXT DAYS
AND WEEKS, THE LITTLE
ELEPHANT BECAME NOT
JUST PART OF THE FAMILY,
BUT PART OF THE
VILLAGE LIFE
Signed and dated 2021
Watercolour and pencil
16 ½ × 18 ½ INCHES

281 *(opposite below)*
SOMETIMES HE
FOLLOWED NOA TO
SCHOOL AND JOINED IN
THE PLAYGROUND GAMES
Signed and dated 2021
Watercolour and pencil
10 ½ × 20 INCHES

283

ONE NIGHT, THERE WAS A TREMENDOUS STORM. IT WAS THE BEGINNING OF THE RAINY SEASON AND ALL NIGHT LONG THUNDER BOOMED AND LIGHTNING FLASHED

Signed and dated 2021

Watercolour and pencil

9 ½ × 8 ¾ INCHES

284

THE NEXT MORNING, THE RIVER WAS RUSHING AND ROARING AND BURSTING OVER THE BANKS. NOA RAN TO MAKE SURE THAT HIS BOAT WAS SAFE FROM THE FLOODWATER

Signed and dated 2021

Watercolour and pencil with bodycolour

11 × 7 ¾ INCHES

285
SUDDENLY TEMBO EMERGED FROM THE RIVER BELOW HIM. HE HAD
BEEN THE 'SOMETHING SOLID' BENEATH NOA'S FEET
Signed, inscribed with book title below mount and dated 2021
Watercolour and pencil with bodycolour
10 ¼ × 16 INCHES

286
THE LITTLE ELEPHANT SPLASHED NOA
Signed, inscribed with title below mount and dated 2021
Watercolour, pencil and bodycolour
10 ¼ x 10 INCHES

287
MOTHER AND BABY ELEPHANT
Signed, inscribed 'Noa' below mount and dated 2021
Watercolour and pencil
11 x 7 ¾ INCHES
Illustrated: back cover

PETER CROSS
Peter Cross (born 1951)

From 1975, Peter Cross began to emerge as an illustrator of great originality, making his name with books that continue to delight children and adults alike. Unwilling to restrict his fertile imagination to two dimensions, he also created a series of eccentric cabinets of curiosities. Such richness and variety were then directed towards advertising and, in particular, to delightful work for the company Wine Rack. Cross's dry, yet charming visual-verbal wit has reached a wide international public through designs for greetings cards, first for Gordon Fraser (Hallmark 1995-2000) and then for The Great British Card Company.

For a biography of Peter Cross, please refer to *The Illustrators*, 2018, page 150

289
THE ILLUSTRATORSSSSS
Signed with initials and dated 2022
Watercolour and pencil
4 ¾ × 4 INCHES

288 *(below left)*
FROM DINOSAURS TO DORMICE
Signed with initials
Ink and watecolour
5 ¼ × 4 INCHES

290
MOTORISED GOLF SHOES
Signed with initials and inscribed with title
Watercolour with bodycolour
8 × 7 ¼ INCHES

291
HARBOTTLE'S BEER KEEPIE-UPPIE
Signed with initials and inscribed with title
Watercolour with pencil
5 ¼ × 3 ¼ INCHES

292
CUPBOARD LOVE
Signed with initials and inscribed with title
Watercolour with pencil
4 × 3 INCHES

293
BAROL SINGING
Signed with initials and inscribed with title
Watercolour and bodycolour
6 ¾ × 4 ¾ INCHES

294

SOCIAL BUBBLES
Signed with initials and inscribed with title
Watercolour with pencil
5 ¼ x 4 ¼ INCHES

295

MERRILY WE GO...
ROUND THE CHRISTMAS TREE!
Watercolour
5 ¾ x 4 ¼ INCHES

296

HOW TO MAKE CAT BAUBLES
Signed with initials twice
Watercolour with bodycolour
9 ¼ x 11 ¾ INCHES

AMANDA HALL
Amanda Hall (born 1956)

Amanda Hall is an award-winning contemporary illustrator, particularly renowned for her wonderfully decorative and colourful children's book illustrations, as well as her work for educational publications both in Britain and America.

For a biography of Amanda Hall, please refer to *The Illustrators*, 2011, page 356

Nos *297-304* are all illustrated in Dawn Casey, *Little Bear: An Inuit Folktale*, Bloomington, Indiana: Wisdom Tales, 2022

Amanda Hall, has over the last two years produced an abundance of new work.

Little Bear: An Inuit Folktale, published in 2022 by Wisdom Tales, is her latest illustrated picture book; her second collaboration with children's author, Dawn Casey (following *Babushka* in 2015). It is a deeply sensitive story based on an Inuit folktale; Amanda Hall has captured the warmth of the characters in the story, whilst also exquisitely depicting the snow-covered arctic landscape through the mediums of watercolour ink and soft pastel pencil.

Amanda Hall has just completed the illustrations for Jennifer Berne's book *How the Sea Came to Be*, an evolutionary tale of sea. The book will be published in April 2023 by Eerdmans Books for Young Readers. The Chris Beetles Gallery will launch this beautiful book and display all the remarkable artwork in a selling exhibition in April 2023.

297
WHEN SHE SLEPT, THE BEAR CUB SLEPT BESIDE HER. AND THE CUB GREW
Signed
Watercolour ink with coloured pencil
7 ½ x 9 ½ INCHES

298
KU LU, MY LITTLE ONE,
MY LITTLE BEAR, MY SON
Signed
Watercolour ink with coloured pencil
11 ½ × 13 ¼ INCHES

299
SHE SAW A SCRAP OF FUR. NO, NOT A
SCRAP – IT WAS SHIVERING, SQUEAKING.
A BEAR CUB
Signed
Watercolour ink with coloured pencil
12 ½ × 23 ½ INCHES

300
THE MEN OF THE VILLAGE
PLAYED WITH THE BEAR,
PRACTICING THEIR SPORTS
WITH HIM
Signed
Watercolour ink with coloured pencil
6 x 12 ½ INCHES

301
AN OLD WOMAN LIVED
BY HERSELF, AND WAS
LONELY
Signed
Watercolour ink with coloured pencil
11 x 13 INCHES

302

BY SPRING, WHEN THE DAYS LENGTHENED AT LAST,
THE BEAR COULD CATCH SALMON AND SEAL BY HIMSELF
Signed
Watercolour ink with coloured pencil
11 ½ x 13 INCHES

303

"LITTLE BEAR", SHE PUT HER ARMS AROUND
HIS NECK AND HER TEARS RAN INTO HIS FUR.
"BEARS BELONG IN THE WILD. GO. BE FREE ..."
Signed
Watercolour ink with coloured pencil
11 x 12 INCHES

304

SHE PUTS HER ARMS AROUND HIS
NECK, AND THEY NUZZLE
Signed
Watercolour ink with coloured pencil
11 ½ x 21 ½ INCHES

Paul Cox

PAUL COX

PAUL COX
Paul William Cox (born 1957)

Paul Cox's fluid, immediate draughtsmanship and vibrant colour make him one of the most enjoyable, versatile and sought-after of contemporary illustrators. Well known for his warm and witty contributions to books and magazines, he has ranged in his work as a designer from stamps to stage sets.

Paul Cox was born in London in 1957, the eldest child of architect Oliver Cox CBE, he was raised in Dorset and Hampshire. Paul Cox studied illustration at Camberwell College of Art and then at the Royal College of Art. After graduating in 1982 he worked as a freelance artist, earning success for his distinctive and lively style of illustration and his work is easily recognised on the pages of the *Daily Telegraph*, *Country Life*, *The Spectator*, *The Sunday Times Magazine*, *Punch*, *The Times*, *Blueprint Magazine*, *Vanity Fair* and *Esquire*.

In 1984 Paul Cox began a close professional relationship with the Folio Society, leading to book illustrations that highlight both the warmth and wit of his work. Volumes include: Jerome K Jerome's *Three Men in a Boat* (1992) and 17 novels by P G Wodehouse. In 2006, he illustrated the 50th anniversary version of Gerald Durrell's *My Family and other Animals*. These illustrations formed two exhibitions at the Durrell Wildlife Foundation, Jersey and Chris Beetles Gallery, London.

Chris Beetles held the first major retrospective of Paul Cox's work in 2001, with another in 2013 accompanied by the book *A Journey Through His Art*. In 2011 Paul Cox moved back from Sussex to his beloved capital:

> I have always loved London. I think its in my blood, and I recognise, belatedly, perhaps, that it was somewhere I shouldn't have left, but I'm glad I had, because I appreciate it more.

It is the city that has inspired much of his work, amongst the vivid depictions of life in Paris, Rome, and New York.

In 2020 he illustrated *The Short, The Long and The Tall*, a limited-edition collection of short stories by best-selling novelist Jeffrey Archer. Paul Cox involves himself with a variety of these collaborative works, including stamp designs for the Royal Mail, set designs for the 50th anniversary production of the musical, *Salad Days*, a mural for the lecture hall at the Royal College of Surgeons, and a variety of work in the States.

Most recently he has completed a series of work exploring the London pubs drawn and frequented by Edward Ardizzone. He continues to live in Highgate with his wife, with whom he has two children.

FOLLOWING IN ARDIZZONE'S FOOTSTEPS
By Robert Bruce

It does seem extraordinary. But if you walk around the area of Maida Vale where Edward Ardizzone lived for most of his life the pubs which he so enjoyed and drew incessantly are largely still there. It is perfectly possible to follow in his footsteps and enjoy the beer, the architectural glories, and the amiable humanity he so loved. He lived at the same house on Elgin Avenue, which now sports a blue plaque to him, from 1920 to 1972. He was a disciplined artist and was at his desk by the window early in the morning working on his books, the *Little Tim* series, or posters for Guinness, or book and magazine illustrations. And at lunchtime he would pop down to a local pub. There he would continue his work, his son recalled, drawing the locals on the back of a cigarette packet, or a beer mat, or whatever came to hand. These sketches became his pub drawings. And the drawings became books, *The Local* immediately before the war, and then, the war over, *Back To The Local* in 1949, both written with Maurice Gorham, an old school chum.

This is what this chapter of paintings by Paul Cox commemorates. 'There can be no doubt', Ardizzone's brother-in-law recorded, 'that he found the task congenial and he and the author visited the various houses assiduously'. And that is precisely what Paul Cox and I did on some of the hottest days of the summer this year. We stuck to our task. We would visit the Hero of Maida, in Ardizzone's day called The Shirland, where the winding wooden staircase still exists beneath which in his 1955 etching he shows two delightful old ladies enjoying a drink. We would move to the glory of the Prince Alfred [nos *306-308*] with its many original bars, its curving etched glass windows and its snob screens to enable demure ladies to preserve their privacy while buying a drink, and think how amazed Ardizzone would be to learn that it has just been granted Grade II* listing, the second highest grade on the National Heritage List of England. Then to The Warrington [no *309*] with its huge circular bar and the grand staircase on which Ardizzone depicted 'the girls' in all their raffish disarray. It was the most enjoyable research that either of us could imagine. In Cox's depiction of the main bar in the Prince Alfred [no *307*] his pint of Guinness is refreshingly in the foreground.

Ardizzone's son Nicholas once said of his father: 'It was in pubs he found the humanity that fascinated him, the flawed fallible humanity for which he had such a keen visual sense'. Cox has a similarly non-judgemental and sweet attitude to people and he has added to the repertoire of Maida Vale pubs. One pub, up on the border with St John's Wood, now converted into a private house, was The Alma. It was an Ardizzone favourite. He loved the landlord and landlady, the family atmosphere, and the characters attracted to the pub. One would play his cornet at the door, others played the saw, and one would, for a bet, apparently set up a primus stove and fry and then eat his socks on the premises [no *310*]. As far as we know Ardizzone never drew the scene, but Paul Cox has. Invariably drawing from exactly the same viewpoint as Ardizzone, Paul has commemorated his work from eighty years ago and celebrated the survival of all these extraordinary and joyous pubs.

Please see Edward Ardizzone in chapter 7, pages 117-128

305
THE ELGIN
ELGIN AVENUE
Signed, inscribed with title and dated 22
Ink and watercolour
16 × 11 ¼ INCHES

THE ELGIN

At the other end of Elgin Avenue from their home this would often be a last call on a ramble round the local pubs for Ardizzone, his son and his dog, Toby.

306
THE PRINCE ALFRED
CASTELLAIN RD
Signed, inscribed with title and
dated 22
Ink and watercolour
15 ¾ × 11 ½ INCHES

THE PRINCE ALFRED

Outside the Alfred in the warmth of
a summer's dusk couples gather,
bathed by the interior glow through
the etched and elaborate glass of
the windows.

307
THE PRINCE ALFRED
FORMOSA ST
Signed, inscribed with title and
dated 22
Ink and watercolour
16 ¼ × 22 ¾ INCHES

The artist's own pint of Guinness is
a tempting stretch away. The Ladies
Bar with its snob screens, only
found in one other pub in London,
is at the far end.

236

308

SALOON BAR AT THE
PRINCE ALFRED
Signed, inscribed with title and
dated 22
Ink and watercolour
15 ½ × 11 ½ INCHES

The saloon bar of the Alfred is the
place to relish the elaborate
woodwork around the Ladies Bar
and the towering ornate shelves of
bottles topped by its clock, which
has long ceased working.

309
THE WARRINGTON HOTEL
Signed, inscribed with title and dated 22
Ink and watercolour
16 × 23 INCHES

THE WARRINGTON HOTEL

This is the most epic of Maida Vale's pubs
and this Cox painting echoes one of
Ardizzone's pictures where he depicts
himself, the gent on the right, gazing in a
slightly worried fashion up at the lady on
the grand staircase.

310
FRYING SOCKS AT
THE ALMA
Signed, inscribed with title and
dated 22
Ink and watercolour
7 ½ × 10 INCHES

311
THE BRIDGE HOUSE
WESTBOURNE TERRACE
Signed, inscribed with title and
dated 22
Ink and watercolour
14 ½ x 11 ½ INCHES

THE BRIDGE HOUSE

Nightfall again, here at the peaceful
Bridge House by the canal at Little
Venice. The evening punctuated by
the sharp quacks of coots.

312
THE CLIFTON
CLIFTON HILL
Signed, inscribed with title and
dated 22
Ink and watercolour
15 ½ x 11 ½ INCHES

THE CLIFTON

This is the closest you get to a
country pub in London. In
Ardizzone's day the long building
behind, now occupied by lawyers,
was the home of Carlton Film
Studios where he had many chums.

The Warwick Castle · Warwick Place

Paul Cox 22

313
THE WARWICK CASTLE
WARWICK PLACE
Signed, inscribed with title and
dated 22
Ink and watercolour
20 ½ × 16 INCHES

THE WARWICK CASTLE

Ardizzone depicted two men
walking towards the pub in keen
Sunday morning anticipation. Paul
Cox also shows two men, this time
in the early evening under the
antique illuminated lantern.

ALEX
Peattie + Taylor

ALEX
Charles Peattie (born 1958)
+
Russell Taylor (born 1960)

Produced by Russell Taylor and Charles Peattie, the *Alex* strip first appeared in the *London Daily News* in 1987. It moved to the *Independent* later that year, before finding a home at the *Daily Telegraph* in 1992. The strip celebrated its 30th anniversary with the *Telegraph* earlier this year.

For over three decades, *Alex* has followed the daily life of its eponymous lead, a snobbish, narcissistic, materialistic investment banker and those of his friends, colleagues and loved ones. Occurring in 'real time', the strip has chronicled all the major news stories, global politics and financial crises of the last 30 years.

Russell Taylor was born in York in 1960. He read Russian at St Anne's College, Oxford. His first book, co-authored with Marc Polonsky, was *USSR – From an Original Idea by Karl Marx* (Faber 1986) – a humorous guide to the Soviet Union, which earned him what is still the most vituperative review of his career (in Pravda).

Russell met cartoonist Charles Peattie at a Christmas party in 1986 for the magazine *Direction* on which they both worked. Their first Alex cartoon strip appeared on February 23rd 1987 in the short-lived *London Daily News*. When that paper folded five months later Alex transferred to the *Independent*. In January 1992 he treacherously defected to the *Daily Telegraph* where he has resided ever since. Alex also appears in newspapers abroad and is particularly popular in Australia and, perhaps surprisingly, in Germany (who says they don't have a sense of humour?).

After a brief midlife crisis in the late 90s Russell ran the New York Marathon and wrote a book of his experiences *The Looniness of the Long Distance Runner* (Andre Deutsch 2001). In 2002 he and Charles were appointed MBE for services to the newspaper industry.

In 2007 the pair wrote and produced *Alex* the eponymous and successful stage play, starring Robert Bathurst, which was performed at the Arts Theatre in London. The play toured the world and returned to the West End in 2008.

In 2010 Russell and Charles wrote a ten week drive time show for Classic FM, which was hosted by Alex (aka Robert Bathurst) and shocked and scandalised the station's listenership (many of whom seemingly believed that Alex was a real banker).

Russell moonlights by writing film and TV music (in collaboration with Steve Cooke). Their programmes, mainly very depressing documentaries, have won seven Emmies, seven BAFTAs, an Amnesty International Award and a Prix Italia.

Russell is married to taxidermist, author and promoter Suzette Field. They live in North London with their daughter.

Charles Peattie was born in 1958. He was educated at Great Walstead Prep School and Charterhouse Public School before studying painting at St Martin's School of Art. After leaving St Martin's, Charles began working as a painter of society portraits, but gave up painting professionally in 1985. By this time, he had been submitting gag cartoons to *Private Eye* for a few years and in 1985 he had begun the cartoon strip 'Dick' with writer Mark Warren in the music magazine, *Melody Maker*.

After meeting Russell Taylor in 1986, the pair published the first *Alex* strip in the *Daily London News* in February 1987. In May of the same year, he began drawing the *Celeb* strip for *Private Eye*. Charles would also write the script for the BBC One sitcom series, *Celeb*, based on the strip. The show starred Harry Enfield and Amanda Holden and aired in 2002. In 1999, Charles Peattie would collaborate with Mark Warren on the Grenada television comedy drama *Passion Killers*, starring Ben Miller and Georgia McKenzie. He also wrote sketches for three seasons of the television sketch show *Lenny Henry in Pieces*, which ran between 1998 and 2001.

In 2009, Charles produced a series of animated shows designed for telephones, including an animated Alex strip commemorating the Financial Crisis. In 2012, he wrote and drew the Alex Christmas story 'It's a Wonderful Crisis', which ran over the Christmas period in the *Daily Telegraph*.

In 2014-2015, Charles created animated scenes for the backdrop of a stage adaptation of Christopher Reid's *The Song of Lunch*, which ran at The Minerva Theatre in Chichester, starring Robert Bathurst.

Charles married his first wife in 1988 and married again in 2005. He has two daughters from his first marriage and two sons from his second. He became a grandfather for the first time in 2014.

314 (above)
LAWRENCE IS A HUGE CRICKET FAN, BUT HIS
COMPLIANCE DEPARTMENT WOULDN'T LET HIM ACCEPT
OUR INVITAION TO TODAY'S TEST MATCH
Signed
Ink with coloured pencil
4 ¼ × 14 ¼ INCHES
Illustrated: *Daily Telegraph*, 12 September 2019

315 (below)
MY WIFE HAS BEEN PUTTING PRESSURE ON ME TO GO
BACK TO THE OFFICE...
Signed
Ink with coloured pencil
4 ½ × 14 ¼ inches
Illustrated: *Daily Telegraph*, 3 June 2022

316 (above)
OUR NEW GRADUATE HIRE WHO SEEMED SO BRIGHT AND
KNOWLEDGEABLE TURNS OUT NOT TO BE SO
Signed
Ink with coloured pencil
4 ½ x 14 ¼ inches
Illustrated: *Daily Telegraph*, 7 June 2022

317 (below)
IN A WAY WE HAVE THE PERFECT MODERN RELATIONSHIP
IN THAT WE GET TO SPEND ALL DAY TOGETHER
Signed
Ink with coloured pencil
4 ½ x 14 ¼ inches
Illustrated: *Daily Telegraph*, 27 June 2022

318 (above)
WELL THE RECENT TEST SERIES AGAINST NEW ZEALAND
HAS PRODUCED THREE ENTERTAINING, COMPETITIVE AND
COMPELLING GAMES
Signed
Ink with coloured pencil
4 ½ × 14 ¼ INCHES
Illustrated: *Daily Telegraph*, 1 July 2022

319 (below)
EVERYONE'S SAYING HOW AMAZING IT WAS TO SEE
MACCA AND SPRINGSTEEN ON STAGE AT GLASTONBURY
AND MICK JAGGER IN HYDE PARK LAST WEEK...
Signed
Ink with coloured pencil
4 ½ × 14 ¼ INCHES
Illustrated: *Daily Telegraph*, 4 July 2022

320 *(above)*
IN A WAY IT'S GOOD THAT WE PUT OFF GETTING
ENGAGED UNTIL NOW, CYRUS …
Signed
Ink with coloured pencil
4 ½ × 14 ¼ inches
Illustrated: *Daily Telegraph*, 5 July 2022

321 *(below)*
SO IT'S ONLY THREE WEEKS TILL YOUR WEDDING,
BRIDGET … YOU MUST BE SO EXCITED. WHERE ARE YOU
GOING ON YOUR HONEYMOON?
Signed
Ink with coloured pencil
4 ½ × 14 ¼ inches
Illustrated: *Daily Telegraph*, 22 July 2022

Contemporary
Cartoonists

CONTEMPORARY  CARTOONISTS

MAC
Stanley McMurty, MBE (born 1936), known as 'Mac'

Since 1971, and for almost 50 years, Mac has produced regular cartoons for the *Daily Mail* and then its sister paper, the *Mail on Sunday*. He has always considered that he is essentially apolitical, and that his role is to brighten 'the dreary news copy of the daily paper … by putting in a laugh'. He has achieved this through clear, realistically drawn images, replete with mimetic detail and social comment.

Stan McMurtry was born in Edinburgh on 4 May 1936, the son of the commercial traveler, Stanley McMurtry, and his wife, Janet. When he was about the age of 10, he moved with his family to Solihull in Warwickshire, and was educated locally at Sharmans Cross High School for Boys.

Between 1950 and 1953, McMurtry studied at Birmingham College of Arts and Crafts. Then, having undertaken National Service in the Royal Army Ordnance Corps (1954-56), he moved to Henley-on-Thames, in Oxfordshire, to begin work at Nicholas Cartoon Films, an animation production company newly established by Nicholas and Mary Spargo. By the time of his first marriage, to Maureen Flaye in 1958, he had become one of the company's key animators, and would work on two films that won awards at the Cannes Film Festival. He and Maureen would have one son and two daughters. During his spare time, he began to produce gag cartoons, which he would send to newspapers and magazines, in the hope of their being accepted. Eventually, he had a cartoon published in *Today* on 7 January 1961.

In 1965, McMurtry left Nicholas Cartoon Films in order to establish himself as a freelance cartoonist. While continuing to contribute cartoons to periodicals, such as *Punch* and the *London Evening News*, he also drew strips for children's comics, including 'Percy's Pets' for *Smash* and 'Pest of the West' for *Wham!*

In 1968, McMurtry became the topical cartoonist for the *Daily Sketch* (on the retirement of Norman Mansbridge), and from January 1969 produced a daily cartoon, which he signed 'Mac'. When the *Daily Sketch* was absorbed by the *Daily Mail* in 1971, the editor, David English, chose McMurtry over the *Daily Mail*'s existing political cartoonist, Wally Fawkes. McMurtry then worked in tandem with John Musgrave-Wood (who signed as 'Emmwood'), until Musgrave-Wood retired in 1975. From that year, McMurtry drew five cartoons a week, with John Kent contributing the sixth, then from 1979 drew four a week. From 1978, his cartoons were collected in annuals, and later celebrated

in two volumes edited by Mark Bryant: *25 Years of Mac* (1996) and *50 years of Mac* (2018).

During the 1970s, McMurtry also collaborated with Bernard Cookson on comedy scripts for Dave Allen and Tommy Cooper (1973-76), and produced a children's book, *The Bunjee Venture* (1977), which provided the source for four animated cartoons by Hanna-Barbera (1984-85).

Having divorced his first wife in 1980, McMurtry married Janet Rattle in Maidstone, Kent, in the following year. From that time, he regularly incorporated her likeness into his cartoons. Then, two decades later, in 2003, when he married his third wife, Elizabeth Vaughan, in Kensington, her likeness began to replace that of Janet.

During the 1980s, McMurtry began to receive the first of many awards. Most notably, the Cartoonists' Club of Great Britain voted him Social and Political Cartoonist of the Year (1983, 1984), Cartoonist of the Year (1983, 1988) and Master Cartoonist (2000); the UK Press Gazette named him Cartoonist of the Year (1982, 1984, 1999); the What the Papers Say Awards named him Cartoonist of the Year (2003, 2007); the Cartoon Art Trust named him Political Cartoonist of the Year (2007) and presented him with a Lifetime Achievement Award (2010); and the Society of Editors named him Cartoonist of the Year (2016, 2018). In 2004, he was appointed a Member of the Order of the British Empire. A member of several clubs, he was Chairman of the Saints and Sinners for the year 2015-16.

McMurtry retired from the *Daily Mail* in 2018, in the year following the death of his third wife, Liz. However, he came out of retirement in December 2020 to work for the *Mail on Sunday*.

His work is represented in the collections of the British Cartoon Archive, University of Kent (Canterbury).

322

OVER THERE, HAMISH. THE STRANGE CREATURES WITH BUMPS ON THEIR CHESTS, LONG HAIR AND NO TROOSERS. I THINK THEY MUST BE THOSE WOMEN THINGS WE'VE HEARD ABOUT

Signed and inscribed with title
Ink and watercolour with bodycolour
15 × 22 INCHES
Illustrated: *Daily Mail*, 15 March 2017

323

THAT'SH IT. NO MORE DRINKING! HAVE YOU MADE ANY NEW YEAR RESHOLUTIONS, VERA?

Signed and inscribed with title
Ink and watercolour with bodycolour
14 ¾ × 19 ¾ INCHES
Illustrated: *Daily Mail*, 1 January 2015

324

ALL THAT DRILLING AND
BANGING. I EXPECT ANGUS
NEXT DOOR IS MAKING
ANOTHER OF HIS ENERGY
SAVING DEVICES.
Signed and inscribed with title
Ink and watercolour
15 × 20 INCHES
Illustrated: *Daily Mail*, 2 August 2017

325

WELL. HERE'S A LAUGH. IT SAYS
ON THE MENU 'GROPING IS AT
YOUR OWN RISK'
Signed and inscribed with title
Ink and watercolour with bodycolour
14 ¾ × 19 ¾ INCHES
Illustrated: *Daily Mail*, 25 January 2018

326

SCOFF ALL YOU LIKE. IT'S MY
DUTY AS PRESIDENT OF HIS
FAN CLUB TO ARRANGE LITTLE
SURPRISES LIKE THIS

Signed and inscribed with title
Ink and watercolour with bodycolour
14 ¾ × 20 INCHES
Illustrated: *Mail on Sunday*, 19 December
2020, 'Mac is back!' (article announcing
Mac's return from retirement)

327

OH NO! HAPPY AND SLEEPY
MUST HAVE HAD LINKS WITH
THE SLAVE TRADE!

Signed and inscribed with title
Ink and watercolour
14 ¾ × 19 ¾ INCHES
Illustrated: *Mail on Sunday*, 19 December
2020, 'Mac is back!' (article announcing
Mac's return from retirement)

MIKE WILLIAMS
Michael Charles Williams (born 1940)

Since his first cartoon was published in *Punch* in 1967, Mike Williams has contributed regularly to many periodicals. His technically confident watercolour images have an immediate charm, but can also be darkly humorous. He has a particular interest in comic representations of animal life, which he calls his 'Animalia', and of historical events.

For a biography of Mike Williams, please refer to *The Illustrators*, 1999, page 245.

328 (above)
NOW DO YOU BELIEVE ME?
Signed
Ink and watercolour
10 x 13 ¾ INCHES

329 (above right)
RECYCLING
Signed
Ink and watercolour
9 x 13 INCHES

330 (right)
... NO BUT SERIOUSLY ...
Signed and inscribed with title
Ink and watercolour
12 x 15 ½ INCHES

ED MCLACHLAN
Edward Rolland McLachlan (born 1940)

Widely regarded as one of the greatest living English cartoonists, Ed McLachlan offers a comical but often cutting commentary on modern life. From his gormless, baggy-suited businessmen to his ungainly bucktoothed women, his undeniably British sense of humour makes him a master of the macabre with an eye for the ridiculous. In every cleverly observed image, he takes the mundane and delivers the hilariously absurd.

For a biography of Ed McLachlan, please refer to *The Illustrators*, 2002, page 110.

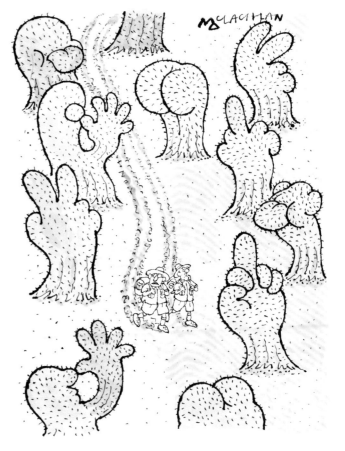

331 (above)
COBBERDOG
AUSTRALIA'S NO1 DOG
WALKING SERVICE
Signed
Ink and watercolour
7 ½ × 10 ½ INCHES
Illustrated: *The Oldie*,
issue 414, June 2022

332
I MUST SAY, THIS IS THE MOST HOSTILE
DESERT I'VE EVER EXPERIENCED
Signed and inscribed with title
Ink and watercolour
13 ½ × 9 INCHES
Illustrated: *The Oldie*, issue 414, June 2022

333 (left)
DE RAMBOIS SCHOOL OF BALLET
Signed
Ink with watercolour
7 ½ × 8 ¾ INCHES
Illustrated: *The Oldie*, issue 415, July 2022, page 67

334

HE DIDN'T WANT TO GO ON HOLIDAY WITH HIS FAMILY
THIS YEAR SO THEY TOOK THE DOG INSTEAD
Signed and inscribed with title
Ink with watercolour
10 × 16 ¼ INCHES
Illustrated: *The Oldie*, issue 416, August 2022, page 92

335

WITH THE EXORBITANT PRICE OF SCHOOL
UNIFORMS NOW, HIS NEW OUTFIT HAS GOT
TO LAST HIM UNTIL HE LEAVES
Signed and inscribed with title
Ink and watercolour; 8 × 9 ½ INCHES
Illustrated: *Private Eye*, issue 1582, 23 September 2022, page 33

336
NOW THAT'S WHAT
I CALL REAL NORTHERN
LIGHTS!
Signed
Ink and watercolour
10 ¼ × 16 ¼ INCHES
Illustrated: *The Oldie*, issue 412,
April 2022, page 63

337
I CAN'T WAIT TO MEET HIM – I WAS TOLD
HE IS A SELF-MADE MAN
Signed and inscribed with title
Ink and watercolour
9 × 10 ½ inches
Illustrated: *The Oldie*

338
NO SNAIL WAS KEPT IN THIS SHELL OVERNIGHT
Signed and inscribed with title
Ink with watercolour
8 ¼ × 14 ½ inches
Illustrated: *The Oldie*

339
DO TELL ME IF I'M BORING YOU
Signed
Ink and watercolour
9 ½ × 13 ¾ inches
Illustrated: *The Oldie*, issue 415, July 2022,
page 44

PETER BROOKES
Peter Derek Brookes, CBE FRSA RDI (born 1943)

*'His target is rarely the ideology of one politician or another. It is the vanity,
inanity and mediocrity of the whole damn lot.'*
(Matthew Parris, *The Times*, 13 October 2009)

Peter Brookes maintains the most consistently high standard of any editorial cartoonist working in Britain today. His daily political cartoons and regular 'Nature Notes', produced for *The Times*, are always inventive, incisive and confidently drawn. They are the fruit of wide experience as a cartoonist and illustrator, and of complete independence from editorial intrusion.

For a biography of Peter Brookes, please refer to *The Illustrators*, 2009, page 164.

His work is represented in the collections of the British Cartoon Archive (University of Kent).

340
WRECKING BALL...
Signed and dated '11 xii 21'
Ink and watercolour
8 × 11 INCHES
Illustrated: *The Times*, 11 December 2021

341
'Z' IS FOR ZELENSKY
Signed and dated '9 iii 22'
Ink and watercolour
8 × 11 INCHES
Illustrated: *The Times*,
9 March 2022

342
WORRIED ABOUT PETROL
PRICES? TRY THESE
Signed and dated '2 iv 22'
Ink and watercolour
8 × 11 INCHES
Illustrated: *The Times*, 2 April 2022

343
FAMILY BUTCHER ...
Signed and dated '6 iv 22'
Ink and watercolour
8 × 11 INCHES
Illustrated: *The Times*, 6 April 2022

344
THIS WAR COULD LAST
YEARS, PRIME MINISTER
Signed and dated '29 iv 22'
Ink and watercolour
8 × 11 INCHES
Illustrated: *The Times*, 29 April 2022

345
HIS MASTER'S VOICE
Signed, inscribed 'with acknow-
ledgements ...' and dated '28 ix 22'
Ink and watercolour
8 × 11 INCHES
Illustrated: *The Times*,
28 September 2022

346
AH, BOND MARKETS ... I'VE
BEEN EXPECTING YOU!
Signed and dated '24 ix 22'
Ink and watercolour
8 × 11 INCHES
Illustrated: *The Times*,
24 September 2022

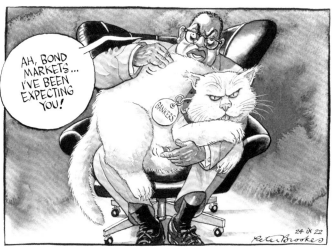

MATT
Matthew Pritchett, MBE (born 1964), known as 'Matt'

'His genius lies in being witty without being nasty'

(Charles Moore, quoted in Max Davidson, *Daily Telegraph*, 17 October 2008)

Matt's much-loved pocket cartoons provide a consistently original take on the big news stories of the day.

For a biography of Matt, please refer to *The Illustrators*, 2009, page 185.

Nos *347-356* are all signed, executed in ink and are illustrated in the *Daily Telegraph*.

347

I'M TRYING TO ORGANISE AN AIRLIFT TO GET BORIS OUT OF WESTMINSTER BEFORE SOMETHING AWFUL HAPPENS

4 × 3 INCHES

Illustrated: Thursday 27 January 2022

348

I'VE GOT OUR NEW FIXTURE LIST. WE PLAY CHINA, THEN CHINA, FOLLOWED BY CHINA, CHINA AND CHINA …

4 × 3 INCHES

Illustrated: Tuesday 1 March 2022

Matt Pritchett, *Matt 2022*, London: Seven Dials, 2022

349

GET THIS OVER TO FORENSICS

4 × 3 INCHES

Illustrated: Wednesday 26 January 2022, inside cartoon

350

THEY SAY SOME ANIMALS CAN SENSE WHEN A RISE IN INTEREST RATES IS IMMINENT

4 × 3 INCHES; Illustrated: Friday 6 May 2022

351

A RATINGS AGENCY
DOWNGRADED MY HAT

5 × 4 INCHES
Illustrated: Friday 22 June 2012

352

THOSE AREN'T TEARS OF JOY AT
SEEING YOU, HE'S BEEN READING
AN ECONOMIC FORECAST

4 × 3 INCHES
Illustrated: Wednesday 24 August 2022

353

I'M PLEASED YOU'RE ALL ENJOYING
OUR CENTRAL HEATING, BUT WOULD
SOMEBODY PLEASE BUY A DRINK?

4 × 3 INCHES
Illustrated: Saturday 3 September 2022

354

DEDICATED TO THE RUSSIAN
TROOPS IN UKRAINE

4 × 3 INCHES
Illustrated: Tuesday 13 September 2022,
inside cartoon

355

ISAAC NEWTON DISCOVERS
THEY'RE FRACKING NEARBY

4 × 3 INCHES
Illustrated: Friday 23 September 2022

356

THIS IS YOUR TORY MP. FORGET
EVERYTHING I'VE SAID FOR THE
PAST 12 YEARS

4 × 3 INCHES
Illustrated: Saturday 24 September 2022

JONATHAN CUSICK
Jonathan Kristofor Cusick (born 1978)

Over the last decade, Jonathan Cusick has gained a strong reputation for his work as an illustrator, and particularly his arresting caricatures, which seem to hold a comically distorting mirror up to personalities who are prominent in the contemporary worlds of politics and entertainment.

For a biography of Jonathan Cusick, please refer to *The Illustrators*, 2010, page 275.

357
LESTER PIGGOTT
Signed
Acrylic on canvas paper
9 ½ × 5 ¼ INCHES
Illustrated: *Radio Times*, 5 May 2001, page 24

358
"SO DO I, I KEEP MINE IN HERE ... FOR LATER"
Signed
Acrylic on canvas paper
12 × 9 INCHES

359
NODDY HOLDER
Signed
Acrylic on canvas paper
9 × 7 ¼ INCHES

360 *(far right)*
DAVID BOWIE
Signed
Acrylic on canvas paper
14 ¾ × 8 INCHES

361
PROFESSOR
BRIAN COX
Signed
Acrylic on canvas paper
7 × 11 INCHES

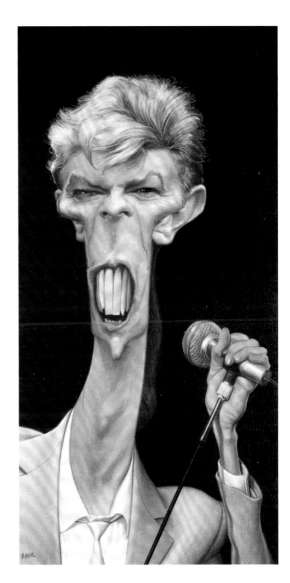

362
BENEDICT
CUMBERBATCH AND
CLARE FOY IN 'THE
ELECTRICAL LIFE OF
LOUIS WAIN'
Signed
Acrylic on canvas paper
14 ½ × 14 INCHES

363
HAVE I GOT NEWS FOR YOU
Signed
Acrylic on canvas paper
14 x **10** INCHES

SELECT BIBLIOGRAPHY

Backemeyer 2005
Sylvia Backemeyer (ed), *Picture This: The Artist as Illustrator*,
London: Herbert Press, 2005

Baker 2002
Martin Baker, *Artists of Radio Times. A Golden Age of British Illustration*,
Oxford: The Ashmolean Press & Chris Beetles Ltd, 2002

Bryant 2000
Mark Bryant, *Dictionary of Twentieth-Century British Cartoonists and Caricaturists*, London: Ashgate, 2000

Bryant and Heneage 1994
Mark Bryant and Simon Heneage, *Dictionary of British Cartoonists and Caricaturists 1730-1980*, Aldershot: Scolar Press, 1994

Clark 1998
Alan Clark, *Dictionary of British Comic Artists, Writer and Editors*,
London: The British Library, 1998

Driver 1981
David Driver (compiler), *The Art of Radio Times. The First Sixty Years*,
London: BBC, 1981

Feaver 1981
William Feaver, *Masters of Caricature. From Hogarth and Gillray to Scarfe and Levine*, London: Weidenfeld and Nicolson, 1981

Horne 1994
Alan Horne, *The Dictionary of 20th Century Book Illustrators*,
Woodbridge: Antique Collectors' Club, 1994

Houfe 1996
Simon Houfe, *The Dictionary of British Book Illustrators and Caricaturists 1800-1914*, Woodbridge: Antique Collectors' Club, 1996
(revised edition)

Johnson and Gruetzner
Jane Johnson and Anna Gruetzner, *The Dictionary of British Artists, 1880-1940*, Woodbridge: Antique Collectors' Club, 1986 (reprint)

Khoury 2004
George Khoury (ed), *True Brit. A Celebration of the Great Comic Book Artists of the UK*, Raleigh, NC: TwoMorrows Publishing, 2004

Lewis 1967
John Lewis, *The 20th Century Book*, London: Herbert Press, 1967

Mallalieu 1976
Huon Mallalieu, *The Dictionary of British Watercolour Artists up to 1920*,
Woodbridge: Antique Collectors' Club, 1976

Martin 1989
Douglas Martin, *The Telling Line. Essays on fifteen contemporary book illustrators*, London: Julia MacRae Books, 1989

Matthew and Harrison 2004
H C G Matthew and Brian Harrison (eds), *Oxford Dictionary of National Biography*, Oxford University Press, 2004 (61 vols)

Peppin and Mickelthwait 1983
Brigid Peppin and Lucy Mickelthwait, *The Dictionary of British Book Illustrators: The Twentieth Century*, London: John Murray, 1983

Price 1957
R G G Price, *A History of Punch*, London: Collins, 1957

Ray 1976
Gordon Norton Ray, *The Illustrator and the Book in England from 1790 to 1914*, New York: Pierpoint Morgan Library, 1976

Reid 1928
Forrest Reid, *Illustrators of the Sixties*, London: Faber & Gwyer, 1928

Souter 2007
Nick and Tessa Souter, *The Illustration Handbook. A Guide to the World's Greatest Illustrators*, Royston: Eagle Editions, 2007

Spalding 1990
Frances Spalding, *20th Century Painters and Sculptors*,
Woodbridge: Antique Collectors' Club, 1990

Spielmann 1895
M H Spielmann, *The History of 'Punch'*, London: Cassell and Company, 1895

Suriano 2000
Gregory R Suriano, *The Pre-Raphaelite Illustrators*, New Castle, Delaware: Oak Knoll Press/London: The British Library, 2000

Turner 1996
Jane Turner (ed), *The Dictionary of Art*, London: Macmillan, 1996 (34 vols)

Wood 1995
Christopher Wood, *The Dictionary of Victorian Painting*,
Woodbridge: Antique Collectors' Club, 1995 (2 vols)

CUMULATIVE INDEX OF CATALOGUES (1991-2022)

C E Brock: [60]

INDEX 2022

· FROM DINOSAURS TO DORMICE ·